RECLAIMING YOUR HAPPINESS

NINE STEPS TO BRINGING MORE HAPPINESS INTO YOUR LIFE

BY DIANE M. KOLODZINSKI

Published by:

The Happiness Clinic
Phoenixville, PA 19460

To schedule author appearances, write to:

The Happiness Clinic
70 Guilford Circle
Phoenixville, PA 19460

First Printing, October 1998
ISBN 0-9667832-0-4
Printed in the U.S.A.
10 9 8 7 6

To my husband, Ray,
whose unconditional love
gave me the strength
to live my life
as the real me

CONTENTS

INTRODUCTION

WHAT IS HAPPINESS

THE MODEL

STEP 1 Commit to Happiness   17

STEP 2 Accept and Take Control of Your Life   21

STEP 3 Accept Others as They are and the World as It is,
            without Judgment   28

STEP 4 Understand Your Needs   40

STEP 5 Realign Your Commitments to Suit Your Needs   54

STEP 6 Live in the Present   66

STEP 7 Transcend Negative Emotions   76

STEP 8 Confront Fear   87

STEP 9 Acknowledge Your Need to Connect   101

INTRODUCTION

Miracles are contained within the pages of this book. The miracle of life. The miracle of living your life the way you were meant to live it. The miracle of change. The miracle of healing, inner-peace, freedom, and satisfaction. The miracle of joy.

The fact that you have discovered this book, opened its pages, and looked within for guidance, is a mini-miracle. You have been inspired to examine your life more closely. You are hoping for more peace, more joy. By wanting it, hoping for it, and focusing on it, happiness will find its way to you.

Your true and profound happiness is a miracle waiting to happen. The tools are within this book. You must commit to joy, know you deserve it, study how to obtain it, and then live for it. It's that simple.

Notice, I say simple — not easy. The process of moving from discontent to peace is not an easy journey. It will take time. You will have to practice. You will have good days and bad.

Like miracles, this book — and happiness — is not for everyone. Some people revel in discontent. They like being unhappy, lost, and hiding. They like to complain, to exonerate responsibility to others, to wallow in sorrow.

Others are more interested in powering over people than experiencing peace and joy. They lack control of their own lives, and so stand over others. They want to be leaders, not equals. They want to be on top, not beside. And in pursuing power, they exchange love, intimacy, and happiness.

Still others are angry and frustrated by something that happened long ago or last week. They cannot face or transcend these feelings and so negativity holds them captive. Happiness cannot coexist with resentment, bitterness, and hate. It cannot thrive in a disappointed, sad, worried soul.

And then there are people who are just scared. They are scared to change, scared to look within themselves. They are scared to do the work that must be done. They are scared of happiness — after all if they have happiness and love and peace, they could lose it, too! For these people, fear holds them in abeyance and blocks their road to joy.

Just as miracles are not for people who do not believe in them — this book is not for people who do not believe in the possibility of happiness. Just as miracles are not for people who are not open to seeing them, this book is not for people who do not believe they can create, foster, and perpetuate joy.

If you are waiting for a miracle to happen, searching for more joy, more satisfaction, more peace — keep your eye on that tiger. If you are ready to face happiness straight on and try new techniques for bringing more joy to your life, read on.

My goal in presenting this book to you is to increase the amount of time you experience pleasure. I want to sharpen your thinking about happiness and put definition around the illusion. I intend to provide you with a model to center your efforts on greater joy.

As a result, you might find yourself spending less time angry, ashamed, frustrated or victimized. You might stop reflecting on the past or worrying about the future. You might stop blaming others for your life. You might become less fearful and more faithful.

Reading this book might encourage you to grow closer to your colleagues, friends, family members, neighbors, and your community. You might stop committing yourself to activities that do not feel right to you. You might find time to do the things that give you the most fulfillment — and not feel guilty about it.

You might discover ways to satisfy your every need, at the least the basics of food, clothing, comfort, and security. You might also pursue an intellectual challenge or stop to walk in the park to reconnect with nature. People around you might become a source of inspiration. You might grow more successful and motivated. You might like yourself more. You might love yourself for the first time in your life.

You might find harmony. You might notice beauty. You might give yourself the leeway to explore life's pleasures, without pressure to perform or do or achieve. You might tap into your creative side.

Finally, you might find it within yourself to make happiness your priority once and for all. After all, when you are happy, the people you love experience that joy with you. When you are happy, you can relax, bathe in peace, live life to its fullest, and share true love.

So, if you look at your life, and you are not happy — 60, 70, 80, even 90 percent of the time — this book can and will change your life dramatically.

Read the wisdom within. Participate in the process, and be open to the possibility of joy. When you do, this book will make a difference. It could be the miracle you have been waiting for. Within these pages, find peace. Find the happiness you were meant to realize.

WHAT IS HAPPINESS?

On the verge of the millennium, in the age of prosperity and technology, where unemployment is at its lowest in a decade, where people are more wealthy and more successful than ever before, why are people so dissatisfied?

Researchers estimate that 66 percent of Americans are happy or extremely happy with their life. That leaves 34 percent either moderately happy or moderately unhappy. That's 95 million people.

Among those, 1 percent of Americans — 2.8 million people — report being very unhappy, possibly clinically depressed. Some estimates put the number as high as 19 million. For these people, happiness is an illusion, a fleeting abstraction.

Society sees the result of this discontent. People — disillusioned and frustrated, alienated and lost — take out their displeasure on others. Crime is rampant, with children killing children. Aggressive drivers use guns to even the score with other drivers who cut them off. Violence, mistrust, and solitude are all around.

In other circles, people walk right by each other without making eye contact or saying hello. The checker at the grocery store barely greets his customer, and people get frustrated because they have to wait for a school bus to pick up children in the morning. On the phone, people answer curtly, assuming the person on the line is a salesperson interrupting their dinner.

In looking at unhappy individuals, we might find that some possess all the outward characteristics we associate with happiness. They had a solid upbringing. They own a beautiful home and work at a successful career. They have a steady income, a two-week vacation every year, and a two-car garage.

Recent studies prove what we have heard all along — that money cannot buy happiness. Unhappiness spans the economic stratum. People living below poverty do, in fact, encounter a higher incidence of depression and sadness. Once above the poverty level, however, income or wealth does not increase or decrease the incidence of joy.[1] Rich people are happy. Moderate-income people are happy. Poor people are happy, too.

With all the abundance that is America — the wealth, prosperity, freedom, choice — why do many Americans feel empty, unfulfilled, and sad?

Some doctors suggest that a physical deficiency — low levels of a chemical, Serotonin — causes otherwise "successful" people to be unhappy. Manufacturers of antidepressants, such as Prozac, and distributors of natural substances, like St. John's Wort, assert these pills increase production of Serotonin, thereby decreasing depression.

Other remedies on the market claim "mood enhancement," greater ability to focus, or increased energy. Doctors are prescribing and people are buying these remedies in record numbers.

Besides the theory of physical deficiency, some theorists believe profound happiness eludes 95 million Americans because our society has such high expectations — expectations that trap us into failure.

Lifestyles on television and in social conversation portray the perfect woman as successful, rich, thin, beautiful, smart, young, sexy, funny, with a picture-perfect home and family life. The perfect man is strong and muscular, a wonderful lover, powerful, successful, articulate, humorous, smart, a scratch golfer, and sports lover.

If we do not live up to these qualifications, we often view ourselves as "less than." When what people expect is perfection, no one lives up to the ideal, and we all fail.

Still another theory about why people are not content is that the media bombards us with bothersome images every day. Our political system is incomprehensible and uncontrollable. We cannot trust our politicians or believe what they say. Companies no longer care about their employees. Violence is commonplace. Can joy exist under these conditions?

All these forces — a chemical imbalance, the images we see, the society we have constructed — certainly contribute to people's unhappiness. On some level, these forces make us all sad.

But, I profess yet another theory. I believe the impetus for unhappiness is much closer to home. I believe the primary source of our unhappiness comes from within, not from external forces.

My theory is that Americans have lost touch with what brings us pleasure. We do not know ourselves and do not understand our most innate needs. We blame others for our life. We resist changing our life to a place that better suits our inner-calling because we are afraid.

As a whole, Americans have lost their inner-selves. We are

busy performing and achieving "success," working more hours than ever before at jobs that often do not fulfill us. Our children are in day care 10 hours a day. We spend money and accumulate debt to buy possessions we don't need. We are exhausted at the end of the day, crash, wake up, and start all over again.

The jobs we hold often do not reflect our true values and our mission in life. Some of us have never given our purpose in life much thought. Or, if we know our life's purpose, we are afraid to pursue it or don't make it a priority. Certainly, we are not living it.

Since we do not understand our mission in life or our true selves, we cannot share openly with others. We have lost intimacy, and our hearts long for love. The divorce rate is more than 60 percent. People have trouble committing and connecting. Some are estranged from even their own family. We don't see our relatives for months at a time and fight around the holidays with the people we profess to love.

Even long-term friendships seem evasive. How many of us spend real, quality time with friends — sharing, visiting, talking openly about our challenges and our successes? How many of us go days at a time without picking up the phone to talk to a loved one?

Our society is mobile, and we have moved away from our communities of origin. As a result, we don't feel connected to our surroundings or our neighborhood, and we don't get involved or volunteer. We don't know the people living right next door. We are afraid to knock on a neighbor's door just to say "hi." Instead, we lock ourselves indoors with security systems.

We entertain ourselves on the Net or by watching television, movies, and videos where the people are larger-than-life and the pace is frantic. We lack face-to-face contact as technology propels us into the fast-paced, Technicolor®, computer-generated, air-brushed, psychedelic world of make-believe and E-mail.

We are too busy to give ourselves time to be creative. We don't paint or draw or color or sculpt. We don't see nature because macadam has replaced grass and dirt. We don't make time to nurture our spirit or our souls. Our life is too hectic, chaotic, and out of control.

There is another way. Some people have found the strength within themselves to conquer fear, solitude, and material accumulation to find genuine peace and happiness. Some people know what gives them joy and have found the courage to pursue it.

Some people have complete control of their lives, their actions, their decisions, and their emotions. They are living life to its fullest — being the happiest they can be consistently and persistently.

These people provide the basis on which this book's nine-step Happiness Model is based. These people inspire us to stay centered, have faith in ourselves, and believe in the possibility of joy.

Components of Happiness

We already know money cannot buy happiness. We also know overpowering others cannot bring us lasting and sincere joy. We know we cannot see joy when our hearts are filled with anger, frustration, resentment, guilt, or fear.

In addition, we cannot sustain inner-peace if we do not take full responsibility for our lives or if we judge and alienate others.

So, what is the true source of joy? Where does happiness originate, and how can we harness it?

Joy does possess a pattern. In studying joyful instances, we see the components of happiness clearly and graphically. Happiness is:

* feeling in control of our destiny. It is working toward a goal and enjoying the process.
* having purpose in life, contributing, feeling a sense of community.
* experiencing flow — being fully engaged in an activity with nothing distracting our attention.[2] It is focusing on what you are doing the moment you are doing it. It is feeling challenged, but not overwhelmed. It is living in the moment,[3] not in the past or the future.
* recognizing and acting on the self with courage. It is identifying what we need and pursuing satisfaction. It is participating in activities that we find fun and interesting.
* accepting love from others and appreciating their point of view, sharing and giving unconditionally.
* confronting fear and moving through negativity. It is being healthy — physically, emotionally, and spiritually.

Happiness is a sign that we are on course. It is a physical sensation, where our heart is pumping, our mind is alert, our sight is clear. We are exhilarated, excited, and at the same time calm, contented, and at peace.

The Whole Self

Now that we know what happiness is, we can discover how to harness it into our lives. Before we look closely at our Happiness Model, however, it is important for us to understand the Whole Self.

Every human being has four main components to his or her being. These components are inner-connected and interdependent. They are:

These components, in concert with one another, encompass a full, complete human being. These components must be in balance — all of them working and flowing together — for us to sustain profound happiness.

If one part of this schematic is off balance, the entire self is affected. I have heard people say: "I am a completely different person at work than at home." At work, the person might be serious, aggressive, tenacious, sharp, and ruthless. At home, she might be caring, considerate, submissive, passive, and lack confidence. This is an example of a disconnection in the Whole Self. It is off-balance.

We are not one individual at work and another on the playground with our children. We are the same human being. We are a Whole Self. If you hate your job, you cannot isolate that part of you and put on a new and happier face at home or in social settings. People sense something is amiss.

If you cannot relax, your love relationships might suffer. You might find it hard to concentrate at work because you are too tired and fatigued. You might question your spirituality, wondering why life is so hard.

If love as passed you by — perhaps you and your partner lack true, clear communication — your ability to enjoy recreational activities will suffer. Your work might suffer, or you might put too much emphasis on work to fill a missing hole in your heart. Again, you might question God or Your Creator about why love escapes your life.

It is difficult, if not impossible, to separate these four sectors of your soul. It is difficult, if not impossible, to turn one part of your life on and another part off. The Whole Self is just that — a whole. Happiness means integrating your Whole Self into one joyful, healthy being.

You might be one of those people who can pinpoint a part of your whole self which is on course or isolated incidents when you were happy. These experiences might have occurred at work, on vacation, during an inspirational church sermon, or making love.

In fact, your happiness might often occur when you are out of your day-to-day grind. On holiday, away from home, in a peaceful setting, where someone else is cooking and caring for you — you feel joyous.

Our goal, however, is to experience happiness 90 or 100 percent of the time — every instance we are alive and in our whole self. We want to replicate the sensation repeatedly — every moment of the day, every day of our lives, no matter what we are doing.

As we study the phenomenon that is happiness, consider the entire being you are. Look at all aspects of your life and see the Whole Self as needing attention. No matter what you are doing — working, playing, doing housework, taking out the trash, sitting in a meeting, or listening to a church sermon — you can realize joy! Now that's a goal to shoot for!

EXERCISE 1 —
Identifying Happiness in Your Life

Throughout this book, you will be asked to participate in exercises of self-analysis. I suggest now purchasing a journal or notebook where you can write answers to questions I ask or thoughts that come to mind as you read. Participating in the exercises will help you incorporate the theories into your life.

In your journal, write down a specific time in your life when you were happy. What were you doing exactly? Who was around you? What physical sensations did you feel?

Go back to your childhood and remember times that brought you the most joy. Examine five-year periods of your life — ages 1-5, 5-10, 10-15, 15-20, 20-25, etc. Pinpoint specific events or activities that you remember as happy times. Try to find one per half decade. Then, ask yourself the same questions listed above.

Can you identify a pattern to your happiness? Were certain people always there during pleasurable times? Did you feel the same each time? How does it feel to remember joyful times in your life?

EXERCISE 2 —
Examining Happiness in Your Life

Look back at one happy experience you detailed in Exercise 1 and review the steps in our Happiness Model as outlined in the "contents" of this book. Pinpoint each of the nine steps as you review that joyful day or incident. Was your heart dedicated to happiness that day? Were you responsible and in control of your joy? Were you judging yourself or others that day? Did you recognize your needs and align your commitments with them?

Were you living in the present? Did you encounter negativity and move through it quickly and concisely?

What were you afraid of that day? Did you overcome your fears? Were you associating with others or nature?

What do you think about the nine-step Happiness Model? Can you see a link between the model and joy in your life?

STEP 1
COMMIT TO HAPPINESS

Several years ago, I looked at my life and thought deeply about what I really wanted. I thought — a new job, a different husband, another child, more money, deeper friendships. I wasn't content, and I didn't know why.

When I continued to ask myself what was lacking in my life, the answer finally came. What I really wanted was what we all want and need. I just wanted to be happy. I yearned for a sense of connection, a purpose, peace, love, and joy.

I started to look at what made me depressed and identified several areas of my life that were off course. I knew what I was doing often did not bring me pleasure. I found disconnects in my Whole Self.

Then, I considered why I was engaging in activities that made me stressed or depressed. Why was I working at a job that was not totally fulfilling? Why was I unable to relax and enjoy life? Why did life overwhelm me? Why didn't I feel a link to my church and my community?

Through this deep introspection, I pledged to make changes to my life. I committed to eliminating activities in my life that did not make me happy. I vowed to replace those activities with tasks that made me feel alive. I promised myself that I would do what made me most happy, and I would be with people who filled my soul with love. I made a choice. I chose happiness.

You might look at your life, too, and wonder why joy escapes you. You might say — how can I endure with all the terrible circumstances happening in our world today? How can I endure with sadness facing me? True — you and everyone else in the world will face challenge in life. We all will encounter pain and fear.

But, commit today to finding joy no matter what happens.

- Yes, we all must die — be happy anyway.
- Yes, our loved ones die — be happy anyway.

- Yes, the world is full of violence — be happy anyway.
- Yes, the world is unfair — be happy anyway.
- Yes, you will get stuck in traffic — be happy anyway.
- Yes, there are mean people — be happy anyway.
- Yes, you are alone sometimes — be happy anyway.
- Yes, you meet with sorrow, despair, depression and loneliness — be happy anyway.

All these "bad" circumstances exist in our world. But, "good" circumstances and love exist also. While death exists, life does, too. While crime exists, healing is present. While the world can be violent, many people also share love and affection toward one another. While the world is unfair, justice often prevails.

Do not overlook the positive. If you believe life is sad, hurtful, and tragic, life is just that. If you believe life is filled with joy and wonder, life will be just that. If you believe you cannot be happy, you cannot. If you believe you can, you can and will.

EXERCISE 3 — Roadblocks to Your Happiness

List some roadblocks in your pursuit of happiness. What is holding you back in life from experiencing joy? What are you currently making more important than your joy?

What tragedies have you faced in your life and how did and do they affect you? Reflect on what brings you down about your life and the world around you. When do you feel sorrow, hurt, pain and/or misery?

For each tragedy or sorrowful experience you listed above, also write down a joy that might or has resulted from that event.

For example, if a relative died recently, can you recall other people to whom you grew closer because of this person's death? If you recently lost your job, can you think of an opportunity that surfaced because of this change?

If you are experiencing abuse or pain right now, what can you imagine is the purpose of that abuse or pain? What can you see that could give you hope that happiness is possible?

As a runner, I often think about running five miles as a metaphor for life. As you run, some roads are flat, some are uphill, some are downhill. When the path escalates, you face a physical battle to muster every bit of strength within you to make it to the top. When the path is downhill, you cruise, pick up speed, or rest until the next hill.

Throughout the journey, you can choose to push yourself or jog leisurely. You can stop, take a rest, then continue. You can stop completely and start over another day. You can completely give up.

Life is a five-mile run. You have alternatives — to enjoy or resist — at every step. You can savor every part of the journey, uphill or down. Or, you can complain and add to your burden along the way.

Like running five miles, creating more happiness in your life will take commitment, focus, and determination. A commitment is a promise — to yourself or someone else — that you will give a challenge your best effort and see to its end. It is a pledge that you will complete a task — you will try your best.

Pledge now to face the decisions you have to make to move forward in your life. Pledge now to embark on the journey of rediscovering peace. Know that profound happiness is feasible. Profound happiness is within your reach, if you choose to see it.

In *Baby Steps to Happiness*, John Q. Baucom speaks of change and the pursuit of happiness. He says that if you want to keep being miserable, keep doing what you are doing. If not, "do things differently. If something you're doing is not working for you, change it. Don't do the same thing over and over and expect different results."[4]

Try something new, and eventually, you will stumble upon what makes you happy.[5] To find joy, change is inevitable. If you are not ready to change, you are not ready for joy. Put this book away and come back to it when you are ready. The challenge of retooling your life awaits you.

To be happy, make happiness a priority. Work to obtain it. Study the components of it and pursue it as a goal, just as you would a job, a partner, money, or fame. Now — before you read any further — pledge to yourself that experiencing more pleasure is your number one goal. Make happiness the number one priority in your life.

In doing so, consider this: you owe it to the universe to be the best you can be. At your best, you can contribute to society what you are meant — by God or Your Creator — to contribute. So, happiness is more than a self-indulgent desire. It is an obligation. The world needs you to be at your best each day.

EXERCISE 4 — Your Commitments

Review current commitments you have with your employer, your family, your parents, and creditors. Observe how your commitments influence how you spend your time — day-to-day. How would your life change if you retracted some or all of your commitments? How would your relationships change?

On your list of your commitments, is your happiness listed? If not, why not? If so, where is it on the list? Can you put happiness at the top of the list, before your job, your family, your children? If not, why?

STEP 2
ACCEPT AND TAKE CONTROL OF YOUR LIFE

Change begins with acceptance.

What a strange idea. After all, if you want to change, you are implying that you do not accept the life you have created. You want to act differently, be a different person, see life differently. You want to eliminate parts of your current life and replace them with more joyful experiences.

Honoring your life as it stands, however, is the first step toward change. You cannot change what you do not see or what you ignore. You cannot change what you do not embrace. You cannot change what you do not take full responsibility for having reared.

Look at your life and all roles you play in your work, your home, your family, your love relationships, your religion, and your relaxation time. See your whole life as a life you have devised for yourself, by yourself. Know that you navigated your life — you drafted it, molded it, composed it, and decided it.

Accept accountability now for every decision you have made up to this point. Know that you made the best decisions you could, given the resources you had. You made mistakes along the way, as we all have. See the "good" decisions you made, and the "bad." Accept the successes and accept the failures.

This is the life you have built. Look at it closely and embrace it as your own.

No One Else is Responsible

Unhappy people often have trouble accepting their lives. They pinpoint others responsible for their unhappiness. They might say, "If I had better parents, I would handle life's problems better."

They might blame a lover, saying that if their mate were stronger or happier or made more money, they would feel better.

Some people even blame their children for their unhappiness. I hear parents say, "If only Joseph would eat his dinner, (clean up his room, perform well in school, marry) I'd be so happy."

At the same time, some parents take credit for the good deeds performed by their children. At 42, a hardworking, intelligent woman earns a Ph.D., and her mother says, "That's my girl," as if the adult were still a child. Another caregiver sees his daughter as a successful lawyer. "I taught her everything she knows," he says.

Though our parents and caregivers influenced us, our accomplishments in life are truly our own. Equally, our mistakes are our own. No one else deserves the credit or the criticism.

Society argues over at what point accountability shifts from your parents taking care of you, to you caring for yourself. Conceivably, that shift occurs at age 8, 10, 15, 18, 21, or 30. Even the law gets involved. Recent cases have indicated that even young teens are totally responsible for their behavior and that their parents cannot be held accountable.

At some point, we all must face adulthood. Somewhere along the way — perhaps between the age of 17 and the age of 22, your life becomes your own. The influence others have is now your choice. You are an adult, and you make your own decisions.

Even as adults, we can and do accept the advice of and are influenced by others. But, influence differs from responsibility. You might seek counsel from others. You might ask for help or consult an expert in a given field. You might even seek advice from your parents or former caregivers.

Ultimately, however, you provide for yourself emotionally, financially, physically, and spiritually. You are in charge of the options you choose. If you are not participating in this process, you are acting still as a child.

We would all like to believe that the people in whose care we were at a young age taught us well. Hopefully, those who influenced you provided a strong foundation on which to build strong life and happiness skills. Often, though, that is not so.

Our parents, like their parents before, brought their own issues to the table. Perhaps they did not have the strength to confront their challenges. They may never have cleaned house on their own life and, therefore, could not help you with yours.

We all live the best we can with what we have available to us at the time. It is now up to you to clean house on your life, despite the model bestowed on you.

If you find yourself blaming your parents, your mate, your neighbor, your friends, your boss, or your children for your plight in life, think again. When you reproach another for your decisions, you project your life responsibility onto them.

Even in the worst cases imaginable — like living in an abusive household — both adults are accountable. After all, if you are being abused, you are allowing yourself to be abused. You are choosing the subservient position and are choosing to release power.

We all know people waiting for someone else to make their life complete. These people put control in the hands of another. Two people specifically come to my mind — a man and a woman — who want desperately to marry.

The woman is a chronic-care nurse, mother to a 5-year-old daughter, and has never married. The man owns a successful business, dates often, has a large group of friends, also has never married.

Both individuals concentrate heavily on finding a partner as their number one goal. Both have told me once they find a mate, their life will be complete. In social settings, they scope the party for a potential partner, constantly searching for Mr. and Ms. Right. When I consider the power these people are handing over to another person, I think: What if he finds Ms. Right, and she dies of cancer! What then?

Looking to another person to give you joy is looking in the wrong direction. If you rationalize that a relationship will make you happy — or a new job, or a new wife, or a new boss, or another child — you are searching in error.

Looking to others only clouds the truth — that you and only you can build happiness in your life. Blaming others for your life or hoping they will change is a waste of precious time. Your time,   and your life.

No one is going to come along and bring you peace. No one is going to give you all the answers in a nice, neat package. You have the answers within you. Happiness is in you and has always been there. Don't give up that authority by looking to another for joy or blame.

And remember — just as no one is responsible for your life, you are not responsible for any one else's. If you spend time trying to make your mother happy, your sister happy, your boss happy, your children happy, your in-laws happy — your happiness suffers. You are not responsible for them.

True adulthood comes when we take charge of our lives — and only our lives. So, stop blaming others for your challenges or giving others credit for what you have accomplished. Stop looking to others for joy, and stop waiting for Your Shining Prince or Princess to come along.

EXERCISE 5 — Clarifying Responsibility

Consider a time when you accomplished a goal you had been working toward for a long time. That goal might be raising two children, earning a degree, getting a job, or excelling in a sport. Now, consider who influenced you along the way. Who encouraged your achievement, and who doubted you?

What were some obstacles you faced reaching your goal? When did you know the goal was within your grasp? Who, if anyone, shared in your accomplishment?

Now, reflect on a time you blamed someone else for a challenge you faced in life. This challenge could have involved marriage, a job, a career choice, your financial situation, or a belief you held. Whom did you blame? Why did you blame this person? How did this person influence you?

Examine your role in both situations. What choices did you make? How did you accept or reject other people's viewpoints? What could you have done differently?

What do you think about taking responsibility for your life? Do you feel responsible for anyone else's life? Whose? Why do you sustain this duty?

Taking Control

You may never have realized the personal power you have over your own life. You might find accepting all of your life difficult. You might endure sorrow about the time you have wasted, giving others power to control you.

That is all past, and you cannot change it. You can, however, influence the present and beyond. Know now that you have complete freedom in every situation you encounter, every task you undertake, every decision you make. Know that the life you construct from this day forward is your life and that you are in complete control.

By now you comprehend the magnitude of having rule over your life. It's mind-boggling, scary, and exhilarating. Literally, we choose everything:

- where we live
- whom we befriend
- whom we marry
- what we do for a living
- when we eat
- when we sleep
- the tasks we perform
- if and when we exercise
- how much money we make
- where we work
- our lifestyle

everything!

Even conflict is optional. Tug of war is a wonderful analogy to conflict. Picture it. One person is on one side of the rope, pulling his hardest to win. The other person is doing the same on the opposite side. If one person — either person — drops the rope, the conflict is over. In any conflict, both people choose the struggle.

Next time you have an argument, remind yourself that you are participating in the conflict. If you choose otherwise, conflict ceases.

We also choose luck or misfortune. Some people believe that others are just "lucky." Many people say I am lucky because I have engineered a life of flexibility. Because I am a writer and own my own business, if I resolve to take a day off to spend with my children, I can.

Other people admire that flexibility and wonder why they cannot create it in their lives. They cannot because they do not take control of what they want.

Lucky people seem to always be in the right place at the right time. Life comes so easily to them. They have a style that attracts fortune and happiness. But, if you ask successful people if they feel lucky, they might tell you otherwise. They will likely say: "I've worked very hard to get where I am. I've made sacrifices. I've learned many hard lessons. I've had good days and bad."

Lucky people have one thing in common. They create coincidence. They create change, and they occasion luck.

We have a choice to be lucky or unlucky. Sad or happy. Rich or poor. Bored or excited. Angry or forgiving. Loving or mean. Truthful or repressive. Living or dying.

Let's look at a case study to illustrate this point.

The Case of Jim

Jim is unfulfilled in his job. An executive with a large manufacturing company, Jim is responsible for six plants in three states. He oversees operations, inventory, shipping, computer systems, profitability, and personnel. Starting as supervisor of an assembly line shift 12 years ago, Jim worked his way up through the ranks. The company named him regional plant supervisor one year ago.

Jim believes he should have been named regional plant supervisor long before last year. He is angry. He waited a long time to receive this promotion. Now, his boss is telling him his numbers are not making the grade. Other regions are more profitable. His labor costs are high, and production lagging. The pressure is on. Jim must hit his profit numbers over the next two quarters or his job might be in jeopardy.

Stressed and feeling the heat, Jim brings his troubles home to his wife. He says even his wife doesn't understand the intensity of this challenge. She doesn't support him. A few nights ago, he talked to her about his job. His wife showed little interest. She told him she was tired of hearing him complain about his job. Her exact words were: "If you don't like your job, do something about it." He thought — "You call that support?"

Jim frequently refers to his job as "boring" and his colleagues as "back-stabbers." When he ponders leaving his company, Jim says to himself:

> *"I cannot find a job making as much money as I do now."*
> *"I have a family to support."*
> *"I know this company is the best in the area. How can I give that up?"*
> *"Things would be better if my boss would leave."*
> *"I've sent out my resume; there's nothing available for me."*

Fear is preventing Jim from moving forward. Perhaps he worries about money, has an aversion to change, or likes the prestige of his current job. Perhaps he is concerned about losing the friendships he has developed at his current employer. Whatever he fears, Jim is putting that fear above his happiness.

At the center of Jim's problem is an even larger issue. Jim is releasing his power to another force. He doesn't recognize that he has the power to stay in his job or leave. Instead, he feels stuck. He is choosing to give up power and, in doing so, choosing misery.

The truth is — you are entitled to nothing in this world. Life is a gift from God or Your Creator. It can be taken away at any moment. Your job is a gift. The money you possess is a gift. Your health is a gift. Your family and friends are gifts.

If you are not content with your life, you must understand God did not promise you roses in your garden. He gave you breath. She watches over you. You are in charge.

If you are unhappy with your life, only you can change it and make it what you want. Don't wait for someone else to act. Don't wait for someone else to give you joy. Go out and find it for yourself.

3
STEP 3
ACCEPT OTHERS AS THEY ARE AND
THE WORLD AS IT IS,
WITHOUT JUDGMENT

Now that you have accepted your life exactly the way it is, it is time to look at others and the world around you.

Just as you fashioned your life, other people have created theirs. It might not be perfect. It might not be exactly the way they would like it to be. But, their life is their life. And, it is the way it is.

Remember, you are completely responsible for your life, and others are completely responsible for theirs. You are the way you are, and people are the way they are. We all, collectively, make up the world. And the world is the way it is.

How you surrender to the facts detailed above directly influences your happiness. If you choose to resist these facts, you will encounter frustration. If you try to change others — an area in which you have no jurisdiction — they will likely become angry and fight back. Conflict will arise.

Whether you like it or not, and whether you accept it or not, other people do not operate the way you propose they operate. Likewise, the world does not operate the way you think it should. Resistance to these facts breeds discontent and unhappiness.

In *The Precious Present*, Dr. Spencer Johnson describes pain as "the difference between what is and what I want it to be."[6] The emotional pain we endure in life often can be linked to this discrepancy.

For example, we become angry when a friend treats us differently than what we expected. We become frustrated with the world when it acts differently than what we intended. We feel frustrated when we fail to accomplish a task we intended to do.

Concentrating on what is lacking in your life, others, or the world around you, can be a source of immense sorrow. By centering on what you do not have or what you did not do, you foster sadness, frustration, sorrow, and sometimes anger and jealousy toward others. Not honoring the world — not honoring what is the way it is — burdens your road to happiness. The good news is that you can release that burden and that pain. By surrendering, you can find peace.

Close the gap between what you want and what you have. Close the gap between who you want another person to be and who they are. Close the gap between what you see as the ideal world and how the world presents itself to you.

In *"Life 101 — Everything We Wish We Had Learned in School — But Didn't,"* John Roger and Peter McWilliams talk about acceptance. "Acceptance is simply seeing something the way it is and saying, 'That's the way it is.' Acceptance is not approval, consent...concurrence, agreement...or even liking what is."[7]

When I think about accepting my world, the one area I feel most frustrated with is my two-year-old daughter. Because she is two, my intellect tells me I can control her actions and her moods — after all, she is a child. But, reality tells me I cannot control my daughter. And, realistically, I don't want to. I intend to celebrate the unique person that she is. That, however, can be frustrating.

As a toddler, my daughter is attempting to gain independence, while struggling with her physical and mental limitations. Her life is frustrating, as she attempts to accomplish tasks she is not ready to master. Simultaneously, she wants someone close by to rescue her when she requires assistance. A parent plays a delicate role in this stage of his child's development — not knowing when to back off and when to press forward.

My child's frustrations are visible at the breakfast table. She cannot yet pour juice in a cup. I ask her to sit at the table and wait for me to serve her. She asks for juice, I say OK, and proceed to the cabinet for a cup, then to the refrigerator. Again, my daughter says, "I want juice."

I say, "I'm getting it." She repeats herself: "I want juice." "I'm getting it," I answer, one more time. She says, "Juice!" Then, again, "Juice!" Finally, I blow my top. "Stop whining," I say. "I am getting it!"

After experiencing this scene many mornings in a row, I struggled to find another way. Finally, the solution came. What could I control? My daughter — no. Me — yes!

I tried another approach. I explained to her the steps involved in getting a cup of juice. I showed her how I walk to the cabinet, locate a cup, move to the refrigerator, open the door, get the carton, put down the cup, pour the juice, put the carton on the counter, and deliver the cup to her.

As I explained the process, she began to comprehend that getting a cup of juice takes time. After a few days, she realized that I was producing her juice as swiftly as possible. She understood that I was not ignoring her and that I was acting on her request.

At the same time, I realized and accepted that at two years of age, she is impatient. She will learn patience, but right now, she does not understand the concept of time. All she knows is that she wants juice, and she has to wait. That frustrates her.

Through this process, I came to understand her better, and she me. Before, we were both resisting or trying to change one another or the situation. Now, we accept each other and our limitations. The result is relative peace. We are both happier.

As adults, we can increase our happiness by surrendering to reality as it stands. We can accept the limitations and abundance within us, others, and the world. Acceptance calms the soul and creates peace. A reality check can help us find that peace.

When doing a "reality check," note what is factual and what is interpretation. Remove the emotion. Center yourself on what is, rather than what is missing. Focus on what you can and cannot control.

After you do a reality check, surrender to what is true about the situation. Accept it completely as it stands. Then, see where you can and cannot change it. See if this process diminishes your frustration and increases your happiness.

As you consider honoring the world, you might say to yourself, "The world is a mess. My world is a mess. There is so much violence, sorrow, and mistrust around us. I don't like the world. I want to change it."

True, the world can be disheartening, and only you and I can change it, since the world is us. We must realize, however, the limitations of our personal power. You are one person, and the world is millions of people. Your impact can be felt, but the masses will produce substantive change — not you alone.

Some of us garnish more power than others to manifest change. The president of the U.S., for example, might possess the power to foster mass change. The head of a major corporation might have power to change the world. A celebrity, with millions of listeners watching her, can influence the world. And, each of us — as a teacher, an author, a parent, a film producer, or an administrator — has the power to alter the world in some way.

But, our individual power is limited. And, before we can

EXERCISE 6 — Reality Check

In your journal, do a reality check on your life. List who you are right now and what you have in your life — the people and the assets you possess. Then, write down some challenges you face.

Read what you have written. Accept your life and what you have accumulated in life as your own. Say to yourself: "This is my life. My life is me. I built it, and it is real."

Take a moment to accept your troubles as your own. Say to yourself — "This is the way it is. This is reality, and I accept it as it stands."

How does this exercise make you feel? Have you ever thought about your life as it stands? Have you been resisting the life you created?

The next time you are angry with another person, ask yourself — what can I do to make this problem better? The next time you are frustrated with a situation, think about what you can and cannot control. Consider:

- How does your anger and frustration block solving the problem?
- How much energy do you consume being frustrated or angry?
- What would it take to change this person and this situation? Do you really want to change it and can you?
- What can you do to remove this anger and frustration from your life?

change the world, we must accept its current state of being. That acceptance is the impetus for change.

Your power to change another person, too, is limited. You might look at another person — a person with whom you spend a lot of time and think — "She is lazy, mean-spirited, rigid. I cannot   live with this person. I cannot live like this. This person has to change!"

In reality, you have little control over her. You can try to force change by making her see what it might mean to her or how her actions influence you. But, you risk alienating her in the process.

Instead, you might consider honoring this person just the way she is. Then, direct what you can direct — you! Once you accept her, you can decide whether to engage her company or not.

The key here is seeing, accepting, and knowing what we can and cannot control. You have no jurisdiction over others. You only govern you and your little piece of the world.

The Plight of Right and Wrong

In any situation, the idea of what is "fair" and "right" differs from person to person. We all hold varying points of view, depending on how we were raised, where we were raised, our past, and our culture.

Every person has preferences — likes and dislikes, and we often label these preferences "right" and "wrong." We have ways we prefer to live our life and ways we prefer to see the world operate. These preferences influence how we dress, what we eat, where we live, when we rest, what job we hold, and who we befriend.

One year, my husband and I traveled to Washington, D.C. to share Thanksgiving dinner with his family. My husband's sister served sweet potatoes. She mashed the sweet potatoes and melted marshmallows on top — browned. They were delicious. My husband commented on how they were as good as their mother used to make.

I liked my sister-in-law's sweet potatoes, but I longed for my mother's sweet potatoes. At my house, my mother would prepare candied sweet potatoes, cut into round pieces, caked with brown sugar and corn syrup. I liked those better!

Whose sweet potatoes were better? Whose sweet potatoes were inferior? Who was right? Who was wrong? Do most people like mashed sweet potatoes or candied? Do most people make sweet potatoes mashed or candied? Which way tastes better to you?

Preference is the key word here. You and all of us have ways we prefer to live — and eat! Are those preferences right, or just right to us?

Preferences influence our satisfaction with an event or a situation. If my husband's sister had served sweet potatoes the way I liked them, I may have enjoyed Thanksgiving dinner more. I may have felt more "at home." I may have been comforted by fond childhood memories.

If we prefer veal to chicken, and the restaurant at which we are eating does not serve veal, we might be disappointed. If we prefer a job where we have autonomy, and our boss watches over us, we might feel uneasy. If we prefer avoiding conflict to facing our problems, we might recoil if someone disagrees with us.

Our preferences taint the world as rose- or murky-colored. We see the world with our preferences as a filter — the world is "good" and "fair" if it acts the way we prefer it to act. The world is "bad" or "unfair" if it counters us.

What happens when we alter our position and accept both sides? If we like chocolate mousse and strawberry shortcake, for example, we might be content when either is available. If we don't mind working with a boss who must be kept informed, we might be less irritated by an overpowering supervisor. If we realize conflict is a part of life, we might feel less frustrated when it happens.

Opening up our preferences — expanding them — can have a positive affect on our lives. Likewise, constricting our preferences, making them more rigid or uncompromising, can magnify dissatisfaction. And, trying to force our preferences on others can cause real problems.

Sometimes satisfying our preferences is essential to our happiness. Some of us, for example, cannot tolerate disorganization in our home. Some of us have to be on time to scheduled affairs. Some of us need to be held a certain way. Be clear about your preferences and when you can and cannot be flexible. Communicate those boundaries.

At the same time, be careful labeling your preferences as right and what you don't prefer as "wrong." Remember, gradations exist between two extremes. We don't have to call conflict "bad" and chocolate mousse "good." Labeling in this way does not take into account that every extreme has an opposite and gradations in between.

If we consider a person lazy, he could also be calm. If a person is loud, she could also be assertive. If we consider a person meek, she could also be kind. An obnoxious person could also be forceful or self-confident.

If we consider a person passive, she could be giving. An unambitious person could be satisfied. A boring person could be content. Notice how the label changes the perception.

Perfectionism

One tendency toward pushing preferences to the extreme — perfectionism — can be particularly hurtful and demoralizing. In *Baby Steps to Happiness*, John Q. Baucom, Ph.D., correlates "right"

and perfectionism. According to Baucom, the calling to be right –
perfection — stems from being reared in a house where love was
based on performance.[8]   If you acted the "right" way, you were
rewarded and you felt loved. If you misbehaved, you were punished.

This authoritarian style implies a "right" way to act or be, and
a "wrong" or flawed way. It also implies that someone who is right
or perfect is better than someone who is not. It implies a "right" per-
son deserves more attention and love than another.

Striving for perfection negates the fine lines between the
extremes of right and wrong, and good and bad. Being right also
denies the varied ways people view and choose to live life.

The interesting fact about perfection is that it is individual.
What I might describe as a perfect day differs from how my husband
might describe a perfect day. My perfect job, marriage, or solution is
in my mind, based on my likes and dislikes, my opinions, and my val-
ues.

The desire to be perfect often leads to indecision and
incompleteness. After all, if I resist making a decision, I cannot make
a mistake and must, therefore, be perfect. If a project on which I am
working is never complete, my performance cannot be less than per-
fect.

Perfection can rob us of process. In striving for perfection, we
look toward an end — when we are finished and the result is "per-
fect." We will see, however, that happiness is a state of being that
occurs in the present. We cannot be happy "then." Happiness is now.

The Case of Arlene

*Arlene decided one spring to make a costume for her daugh-
ter, Kara. A second grader, Kara had been chosen to play the lead in
the school's annual production — Peter Rabbit. Arlene was proud
and wanted Kara's costume to be just perfect. She purchased a pat-
tern and fabric. Six weeks before the play was to open, she started
sewing.*

*As Arlene proceeded, she was not pleased with various steps
along the way. She sewed the side seams twice because the first
seams were not straight. She sewed pink fabric inside the ears but
decided she did not like the color. She ripped the original off,
searched for another fabric, then replaced it.*

*She cut the black outline of the face, pinned it, until she got
the material in exactly the right position, then sewed it. But, when
she held it up, she noticed the face was off center — by a 1/4 inch —*

so she removed the outline and resewed it — the right way.
All this while, Arlene was frustrated and tense. It was now a
week before the play opened, and she still had to finish the rabbit's
feet and belly (the pattern had called for a white belly in the middle
of the brown fur). She also wanted to purchase a white turtleneck for
under the costume. When would she find the time?
Finally, opening day came. Arlene dropped off Kara's cos-
tume at school that morning. She was not happy with the result. She
hadn't had time to sew on the rabbit's belly — it was all brown.
And, the feet were pinned on because she had not sewn them.
Arlene also did not have time to shop for a white turtleneck.
She was going to pick one up that day. She felt overwhelmed and
frustrated. After all her work, Kara did not appreciate the costume
she made. They had a fight in the car that morning. Kara was upset
because dress rehearsal was at 10 a.m. before the entire student
body, and she had no white turtleneck to wear under the costume.
In spite of all the stress, the play opened that evening, and
Kara performed her part beautifully. The audience was thrilled with
the performance, and the children were proud. Afterwards, many of
the other mothers complimented Arlene on the costume. "It's terrif-
ic," said a friend. "What a nice thing to do for the school!" Arlene
replied: "Oh! It was nothing to make!"
After the play, several families were invited back to a cast
member's house for coffee and cookies. Kara asked excitedly, "Can
we go, mom? Can we go?"
Arlene was tired. She had shopped all day for a white turtle-
neck and had rushed to the school to make sure Kara had it for open-
ing night. She ran home to change and get ready. And, while work-
ing on the costume for six weeks, she had neglected other duties
around the house.
She answered: "I would love to, honey, but we can't. We bet-
ter get home." Kara started to cry. "Why, mommy! Why can't we
go?"
Arlene said: "That's enough! I'm tired. It's been a long day.
We're going home, and that's that!"

Each time I read this true story, I become deeply saddened. Arlene's idea of perfection overshadowed her ability to experience joy for herself and for her child. Creating a "perfect" costume became her goal, rather than enjoying the creative process of making something to please her daughter.

Perfectionism also caused Arlene never to finish the costume, since it couldn't be exactly right. She exhausted herself in the process and caused her daughter to miss an event she really wanted to attend. It seems so sad. If Arlene were to lower her perfect standards, would she and her daughter enjoy life more?

If you are a perfectionist, try replacing your desire to be perfect with a goal to feel good about the job you have accomplished. Know that you managed to your abilities and enjoyed yourself, rather than striving for perfection. Focus on what you are doing when you are doing it, rather than the outcome.

In her best-seller *Simple Abundance*, author Sarah Ban Breathnach points out that at the conclusion of creating the earth and all its creatures, the Lord said it was "very good," not perfect.[9] Take heed.

Here's a novel idea from renowned orator and author Marianne Williamson: You are perfect just the way you are.[10] You are a creature of God, and you are perfect, no matter what you do, no matter who you are.

Since we are all creatures of God, we are all perfect. Since the world is us — the world is perfect, just the way it is. What matters in life is not what is good or bad, right or wrong, superior or inferior. What matters is what is.

Being Right and Judging Others

Our preferences and our idea of what is right, justified, superior, and good often influence our opinions of ourselves and others. If another person is not performing a task as we prefer, we see them as inferior, requiring help, or less than us. Sometimes, we even take over the task to perform it the "right" way.

On the other hand, we might see other people's performance as better than ours. They might have a bigger and better home. They might have a more prominent job. They might be of superior intelligence. They might have fame and fortune, where we are just ordinary people.

This view diminishes our worth. It degrades our self-esteem. It puts us on the defensive and makes us wrong. It is hurtful and demeaning.

EXERCISE 7 — Defining Perfection

In your journal, write a brief description of the following:

- Your perfect job
- A perfect spring outfit for a woman
- A perfect woman's body
- A perfect man's body
- Your perfect life
- A perfect spouse
- A perfect home
- A perfect friend

Now, ask your partner or a close friend to write his or her descriptions. Then, answer these questions:

- How did your answers differ? How were they the same?
- How would your definition of a perfect job change if you were to describe a "very good" or a "good" job? How would your definition of a perfect friend change?
- If you were born in a different country, how would your answers possibly differ?
- If you asked 100 people to list their perfect home, how many different answers would you receive?
- What is your perception of perfection? Are perfectionism and your idea of "right" linked?
- What would happen if the world were perfect?

Our judgment of ourselves and others — our desire to label actions or people as "right" and "wrong" — diminishes our joy because it pulls us away from others. We all know people who will sacrifice anything, go to any extreme, alienate anyone — just to be right. We also know people who, no matter how successful they are, still view themselves as "wrong" or "inferior."

Making ourselves right and others wrong — or vice verse — traps us into feeling more or less worthy than others. Sometimes, it feels good to be right or better. Sometimes, it feels good to label our-selves wrong or inferior. After all, if we are "bad" by nature, do we have an excuse for not performing or not living up to standards? Labeling ourselves right and others wrong makes us feel pow-erful, dominant, and superior. Through labeling, we validate how we act or what we do. We justify how we behave and live.[11]

But, these judgments also have a cost. To us, the cost is self-esteem. For others, it's invalidation. For both of us, judgment clos-es an issue to discussion and diminishes mutual understanding.

We cannot live in harmony if we project our preferences onto others with no regard for their beliefs. In doing so, we do not con-sider their needs, opinions, and life experience. We do not live a lov-ing, kind life. Instead, we foster conflict, disharmony, and unhappi-ness.

Being "right" hurts us in the long run. Often, we win the bat-tle, but lose the war. In defending our "right" position, we often push away others.

I often think that passing judgment on another person says more about us than them. Next time you find yourself labeling another person, passing judgment on another, or thinking that you are "right" and they are wrong, think twice. Consider how your judging others is a judgment on yourself.

What is the point of "right" and "wrong," anyway? So, you are right and the other person is wrong. You win. Or, they are right and you are wrong. Now what? Does being right bring you joy? Does being wrong make you feel better? Does justifying your posi-tion give you power and make you feel better? And, at whose expense?

Once we realize that human association and connection is a basic necessity, the desire to be "right" seems pointless. Judgment diminishes comradeship. We might be "right," but we risk being alone.

Next time you find yourself in a discussion over "right" and "wrong," put yourself in the shoes of the other person. Acknowledge that that person's opinion is directly related to his history, his upbringing, his value system, and his culture. See his view as valid. Acknowledge his opinion as real. Respect his point of view. Listen respectfully and consciously.

If you believe a person has treated you unfairly, state your case. Make clear what you expect in the relationship and how the other did not live up to these expectations. Be clear about what you can and cannot tolerate. Listen to the other person's viewpoint on what is fair.

Every person in life needs to be heard, acknowledged and understood. Listening and honoring another's view naturally leads to intimacy and companionship. Compromise is possible. With compromise comes harmony since both people's opinions are valued. We both win. Acknowledging people as they are, without judgment, fosters harmony, love, and happiness. Remove the right and the wrong, and conflict disappears. Instead of arguing, try love and understanding. Celebrate your differences, as they make for an interesting world. Enjoy every person for who they are. Enjoy each instance for what it is. If you accept others and life without judgment, you open yourself to peace. Without "good" and "bad" in the world — without "right" and "wrong" — unsurpassed happiness is possible for all of us.

4
STEP 4
UNDERSTAND YOUR NEEDS

Now that we have taken control of our lives and are letting others live theirs without judging them, we can begin to focus on what makes us happy. Within the context of our lives and the world as it exists, what satisfies us?

Step 4 will uncover the miracle of need satisfaction. We will examine basic human needs and discuss the difference between needs and wants. We will look within you to reveal your true self and learn how you can listen and address your inner needs. And, we will discuss the benefits of understanding, esteeming, and satisfying your needs. Through this process, we will see how gratifying your true and real desires can bring you immense joy.

Basic Human Needs

All humans have needs. These needs are the same, whether we live in western or eastern civilization, are poor or rich, happy or sad, young or old.

Renowned psychologist Abraham Maslow developed a hierarchy chart to classify basic human needs. In the shape of a pyramid, Maslow's hierarchy begins at the bottom with most basic needs — food, thirst, shelter — then progresses upward through safety and security, love, achievement and competence, understanding, and aesthetics.[12]

At the top of the chart is self-actualization, the point at which an individual engages in activities for which she is truly suited. Self-actualized, a person knows herself and acts out her purpose in life.[13]

MASLOW'S HIERARCHY OF HUMAN NEEDS

Self-actualization:
to find
self-fulfillment
and realize
one's potential

Aesthetic needs:
symmetry, order, and beauty

Cognitive needs: to know, understand,
and explore

Esteem needs: to achieve, be competent, gain
approval and recognition

Belongingness and love needs: to affiliate with others,
be accepted, and belong

Safety needs: to feel secure and safe, out of danger

Physiological needs: hunger, thirst, to feel warmth[14]

Needs at the base of Maslow's hierarchy must be at least partially satisfied before those at the middle or top can motivate a person to act.[15]

If a person is hungry, homeless, or lacking love, for example, he will not be motivated by the search for recognition. Instead, his efforts will be spent trying to appease these "lesser" or more basic needs. If a person lacks order and symmetry in his life, he will not be motivated by a desire for self-actualization.

Maslow had his way of terming and categorizing basic needs. You and I might term them differently. Maslow said people need to belong to a group. You might term this "human connection" or "companionship." He termed acknowledgment from others as "recognition," while you might label this "respect" or "attention."

I would add to his chart that people need a sense of purpose and self-worth. We also all need peace of mind.

However we term these fundamental needs, their relationship to happiness is the same. When you are working toward or when your needs are met, you are content. When you cannot find your needs or when you are not addressing them, your happiness is diverted. Satisfying your needs is a key step in realizing profound joy.

Take time now to study Maslow's chart as a source of insight into human composition. While all humans have the same basic needs, we also are born with a unique self and our life is unprecedented. Each of us is at a different stage on Maslow's chart. Each of us has a history we bring to the chart, offering variations on similar or common themes of need satisfaction.

Analyzing your needs and your personal way of seeing, hearing, and fulfilling them can be fun and enlightening. Some of us have never considered what we need or how to fulfill those desires. We are too busy, do not know how to recognize them, or do not comprehend their correlation to our joy.

Before we uncover ways to get in touch with your needs and how to address them, we must fully comprehend the difference between needs and wants. Many people confuse the two, leading them to pursue an object or relationship they "want," leaving them with unsatisfied needs.

Needs Versus Wants

Needs and wants are not the same. As we have seen, needs are basic to our existence. We all have common needs, and we all realize joy through the satisfaction of those needs.

Wants are not needs, though people often mistake them as such. Some people believe that once they obtain what they want, need satisfaction will follow. What happens instead is that our wants actually side track our needs — we get what we want, but our true desires still haunt us.

The Case of Sarah

As long as she could remember, Sarah has wanted a beautiful home. She grew up in a small, three-story townhome in New York City. With six siblings, Sarah seldom had privacy, seldom experienced quiet and solitude. Even the street outside her home was noisy and crowded. She longed for a place of her own.

Once married, Sarah and her husband bought a home in the New York suburbs. They moved from their tiny Manhattan apartment into a three-bedroom cape cod. Two children later, Sarah's home was beginning to feel small. Sarah wanted more space.

She dreamed of decorating her living room to be her peaceful place for solitude. She pictured an elegant room with deep-colored walls, a damask couch, a stone fireplace with a mantel, and two traditional wing back chairs. She wanted book cases to the ceiling and an antique secretary for storing memorable papers. Most of all, she wanted to display oil paintings she had gathered from the many countries to which she had traveled.

When asked why she wanted her living room so badly, Sarah replied: "I need a place that's all mine. My children have taken over my whole house. I need space to myself to sit and read, relax, talk to my husband. My living room is my reward. I've worked hard for many years and now I want what I want. I want a place for me. When I have guests, I want a room where we can sit and talk. I want people to say what a nice job I've done decorating. I want to show my success."

Sarah spends hours perusing home decor magazines and browsing furniture showrooms. Recently, she spent an entire afternoon leafing through wallpaper catalogs.

Her husband calls her actions obsessive. He says she keeps talking about the living room, and the discussion is causing conflict between them. He reminds her of all the bills they have accumulated. With the bills and the mortgage, redecorating the living room is not an option. Spending money now would put the family further into debt. But, Sarah still insists on pursuing her goal, despite her husband's objections.

Sarah insists that she wants (and needs) a living room — her living room. "The money doesn't matter," she says. She is determined to get it and get it now.

Sarah is a typical example of someone who confuses needs and wants. In our case study, Sarah articulated the following wants:

- a nice living room
- a place to relax
- a reward for her hard work
- a room where she can entertain friends
- compliments from her friends
- a way to showcase her success

If you ask Sarah to articulate what she *needs*, she will say:

"I need a place where I can relax. I need a nice living room. I need to be able to entertain people in my home — in a nice place. I need furniture to sit on."

I asked Sarah to read Maslow's hierarchy of motives, then examine her needs. In doing so, her needs become more well-defined. She listed them:

- A quiet place for self-reflection
- To be with friends in a comfortable setting where we can talk and interact
- To feel recognized for achievements
- Self-esteem
- Beauty nearby

Sarah *wants* a nicely decorated living room, but she needs other, less tangible things. She mistakenly thinks that if she gets what she wants, she will have what she needs. Instead, she could address her needs in other, conceivably less expensive ways — in ways that might truly address her inner desires, including connection with her husband.

For example, she could address her desire for a place for self-reflection by setting up a private corner of her bedroom as her space. She could set a table next to a comfortable chair with a journal, books, magazines, and a picture of her family. This corner could be her place for solitude.

To receive recognition for her achievements, Sarah could seek acknowledgment from others or herself. She could tell her husband or parents about her successes, and they might respond with accolades. She could recognize herself for her achievements by purchasing a small, personal, meaningful gift — like a favorite CD or a piece of jewelry.

Does acknowledgment have to come from others? Does reward have to be lavish, expensive, and immediate? Does recognition have to put us in debt?

Sarah could consider fulfilling her needs in ways she can afford. Then again, she might decide she still wants to redecorate her living room. Once she has achieved that goal, she might comprehend that she satisfied her wants, but her needs still exist.

If you center on obtaining wants instead of satifying needs, you might be side tracking your joy. We all want a lot of things in life. Companies tempt us with marketing tactics, convincing us that we need a $120 pair of sneakers or the fastest, newest computer. They convince us we need fine furniture, a shiny new car with a spoiler, cosmetics, and an answering service. We "need" two phone lines, gas instead of electric heat, a lawn service, private school, and hair gel.

Instead of listening to the ploys of others, train yourself to look within for clues on what is essential in your life. Center on fulfilling real and true needs, rather than wants. Pursuing our wants might cost us a lot of money and reap little satisfaction. Centering on needs, however, can bring us immense joy.

You might want a $25 haircut and a $35 manicure every five weeks to keep you in fashion. But, you need to feel beautiful, inside and out. You might want to express anger toward your boss, burst into her office and throw a report you have just completed in her face. But, you need to be recognized and acknowledged for your accomplishments.

You might want a five-disc CD player with remote and a collection of 750 CDs. But, you need music in your life. You might want a house at the beach with a balcony overlooking the inlet. You need to be in touch with nature to restore your soul.

Know the difference.

Uncovering Your True Self

Now that we understand fundamental human needs, let's examine ways to gratify them. Our needs speak to us in subtle ways, and we must learn to listen to that voice inside calling us to action.

EXERCISE 8 — Needs and Wants

Consider an item you really wanted in the past — a new car, a painting, or vacation. Write in your journal specifically what you wanted and why.

Now, go back and read Maslow's hierarchy of human motives. What need were you attempting to fulfill through this item?

If you did purchase this item or do this activity, consider whether the item or action gratified you. Can you list three other items or tasks you could have bought or did to overcome this need equally or better?

In your journal, list 20 things you want right now. Put a check mark next to what you consider real and essential needs. How many needs and how many wants do you have?

Before doing that, however, we must acknowledge that the voice is there and esteem it enough to listen.

If you have not listened to your inner voice for a long time, you have a daunting task before you. You will need to take time to center on what is essential in your life. You will need to uncover who you are, what you need, and how you can satisfy those desires. You will need to find your "lost self."

The lost self is that real self inside that many of us are not aware exists or choose to ignore. Our real self is often concealed beneath the expectations, the obligations, and the hurt we have felt throughout our life.

Our lost self understands basic essentials, but does not feel worthy of acknowledgement or gratification. A lost self is unaware of what gives it pleasure and so never finds it. Often, a lost self will change its mind about its desires, depending on in whose company it happens to be.

A lost self wanders through life with no direction, never quite reaching success. A lost self is selfless. A lost self has no purpose.

You might have a lost self if you were never trained to listen to your true self. Often, our parents or caregivers do not teach us about self-knowledge and self-esteem because they did not command these qualities themselves. A person cannot teach what they do not understand.

Other people feel they should act a certain way or pursue a certain lifestyle to gain the approval of others — our parents, our friends, our spouse, or society as a whole. In the process, we lose who we are. We become someone we are not.

To understand how to fulfill our essential self, we must first find it. Some people spend their entire lives searching for the self they lost in childhood. Others uncover the true self with little difficulty, if they learn to listen to their intuition.

The true self sends us signals, and we can hear these signs if we listen. You might intuitively sense that your life is taking the wrong path. You might feel a pull to pursue a dream. You might feel in your heart that what you are doing with your life is no longer gratifying.

Our true self also sends us painful signals if it finds we are not listening. A lost self can disguise itself through workaholism, alcoholism, depression, verbal abuse, anger, substance abuse, or addiction. These emotional pains are a signal that our true self is hidden.

Our lost self can also surface as physical pain, such as an ulcer, cancer, heart problems, back strain, arthritis, or diabetes. Even a common cold can be a signal that our true self is lost and attempting to surface. It is ironic that we call a cold "catching a bug," since catching is an active state. Is it possible that a person must be ready and willing to catch an illness? Is it possible that our lost self is crying out for attention, and illness is a way it gets us to stop and look within for healing?

I would encourage anyone with a physical illness to consider the mind and body connection. Is there a block in your mind, with your true self, that is causing you discomfort? Would releasing your true self ease the pain and the disease?

Emotional pain, resulting in addiction to drugs, alcohol, food, or work, often requires outside intervention to heal. I would encourage anyone with an addiction to seek aid from a trained, licensed mental health professional. These experts are available through private or community resources. Find the strength to ask for help.

For those without an addiction, I would encourage you to look deep inside for your true self. Train yourself to listen to the signals your mind and body are sending. You sense in your body and in your soul if your life is off course. See the signals pointing you to change and find the courage to confront what is holding you back from moving forward.

I believe I lost my true self early in life, only to find it again in my late 20s. Before then, I was wandering through life with no real

purpose, suffering from addictions and mild depression. When the
pain became too difficult to bear, I sought help. I wanted more in my
life. I sought love and connection, peace of mind, harmony and pur-
pose.

In my search for my true self, I read hundreds of books and
listened to dozens of tapes — from Gloria Steinem to Les Brown
and Louise Hay. This study gave me a unique prospective on finding
a lost self and rebuilding self-esteem.

Ask yourself salient questions to uncover your true self. What
makes your heart flutter? What activities can you get lost in for
hours? What do you do that conveys peace? When do you feel most
at home with yourself?

EXERCISE 9 — Finding Your Lost Self

If you have lost your true self or if you would like
to clarify your true self, ask yourself the following
questions:
- If I were to die tomorrow, what would I regret
  not having done in my life?
- If a doctor told you you had only a year to live,
  what are the first five things you would do?
- Pretend you have died, and you are sitting at
  your funeral. Your family, friends, and col-
  leagues are around. Someone has been
  chosen to give your eulogy. What would you
  like this person to say about you? Are you
  living this example today? How can you alter
  your life to move in this direction?
- List 50 things you would like to accomplish
  before you die.[16]

Think about where you found peace as a child.
What were your dreams? Did you accomplish them? Are
they still appropriate today? Were your childhood dreams
yours, or were they passed on to you by others? What
are your dreams now? What would you have to sacrifice
to pursue your life dreams?

Reviewing our past is a wonderful way to reveal our true selves. When examining our history, we remember times and experiences that brought us profound joy. These instances often possess a pattern that unlocks the mystery that is our unique soul.

For me, walking in the woods, being outdoors with no shoes, and jumping in the pool when I was hot and sticky are memorable times. I always dreamed of being a writer. I felt good when I wrote. I felt I had something to say.

My personal memories and dreams provide me with direction today on what I can do to please my inner self. My calling to nature is profound, and I still enjoy hiking in the woods, sitting in the grass, or strolling around the yard looking at flowers. Summer still is my favorite time of year, and I still feel free wearing no shoes!

Writing puts me in touch with my true self like no other activity. I have written and continue to write each and every day. It is so endemic to my soul that a pen feels like another finger on my hand. Without it, I cannot seem to grasp life or joy.

If joy is your intent, listen to your inner soul. It will speak through your senses, your heart, and your intuition. Your inner soul has a language only you understand. Your inner soul speaks so only you can hear.

Listening to Your Inner-Self

While all of us possess the same basic needs, no other person on earth is exactly like you. No one had the same parents and childhood. No one was born the same time you were born to the parents you were born to. No one has encountered life as you have encountered it.

And so, every one of us addresses our basic needs in our personal way. Our true self intends to be heard and calls us to action. Some   people call these messages intuition or instinct. Others view them as "callings." Whatever you term them, the point is to listen and hear.

With practice, I have been able to listen carefully to my true self. After years of ignoring her, I now give her the time she needs to speak to me. I am quiet and breath her into my mind. I surround myself with nature in order to keep in touch with my true self emerging. In doing so, in listening, I have profoundly changed my life.

One area that has changed dramatically is how I spend my time daily. A former workaholic, I now listen to my true self and create my daily schedule around her desires, as they occur to me.

Through listening, I have found a most comfortable and contented routine. That routine is:

6-7:00	a.m.	Wake and shower
7-9:00	a.m.	Play with my children, prepare them for school, eat breakfast
9-12:30	p.m.	Work and/or exercise
12:30-1	p.m.	Eat a relaxing lunch
1-2	p.m.	Rest
2 to 4	p.m.	Work
4-4:30	p.m.	Prepare dinner, eat a snack
4:30-7:30	p.m.	Pick up children, eat dinner, play with children, go for a walk
7:30-8:00	p.m.	Prepare children for bed
8-9:00	p.m.	Relax with my husband, read, work on light chores, exercise
9:00	p.m.	Bed

While this is my soul's optimum schedule, I do not always follow it. Certainly on weekends, the schedule differs, and there are days my soul needs complete rest, a visit with my family, time with my children, or time to wander.

For the most part, though, my life follows this pattern. Morning is the best time for me to engage in a intellectual challenge. I perform my most daunting tasks — editing, working on my business, making significant phone calls — at this time of day. Morning is also my best time to exercise, as it "wakes up" my body and my mind.

My body seems to need an hour or more of rest in the afternoon. Without it, 3 or 4 p.m. is a tedious time, as my body slows down and signals fatigue.

Nutrition is important, as food is a source of energy. I take time during the day to plan and prepare nutritious meals and replenish my body with food. I rarely eat at my desk. I address what my body needs, then come back physically equipped to function.

In the evening, I crave connection or solitude. I enjoy relaxing with my husband, reading, or writing in my journal. Sometimes we play a game of cards or chess. Sometimes, with a new burst of energy, I return to work for an hour or so. After I meet my call to work, I can refocus my mind and body on relaxing and sleep.

Countries around the world have different traditions around eating and sleeping. In Europe, for example, eating a large meal at noon is commonplace. Many people follow that meal with a nap or "siesta" and return to work from 3 to 8:00 p.m.

If you live in western civilization where some people work nonstop 10-12 hours a day, you do not have to embody that level of activity. You do not have to work constantly, day after day, to be successful. I find today I am more successful and happier working during my maximum peak energy hours and resting when I desire rest.

Listen to your body tell you what it needs. It will tell you when to work intensely and when to rest. Meditation is a good way to rest during the day if you work at an office where you cannot lie down. Take breaks when you sense the impulse and return to work renewed.

Invent your own schedule, and forget what everyone around you does! When I worked full-time, I was accustomed to an 8:00 a.m. to 5:30 p.m. work day and assumed everyone worked similar hours. When I altered my job to part-time, I was stunned to see people out and about — walking in the park at 10 a.m., playing with children in the yard at 2 p.m. A whole other world existed outside my office!

You and you alone know what you need when you need it. You and you alone know the unique way to gratify your most essential self. And, whether you think so or not, you are in charge of your day and your time. Center your time on satisfying your needs when they call you to action, and your happiness will increase.

Take time now to gauge your instincts and your internal signals. How do you know when you are tired? Do you know when your body is tired as opposed to hungry? Do you ignore fatigue? When is your mind most alert? Your life will improve and your joy will escalate if you recognize your needs calling you to action.

The more we know ourselves and our essential self, the more we can move toward unlimited happiness. We are responsible for understanding and gratifying our basic needs and cannot look to others to fill our unresolved desires.

Once you begin to hear your true self, work on esteeming it and honoring it. Our true self is not futile and fragile, but worthy, strong, and genuine. Being in touch with our true self and acting on its desires will present us with the possibility of realizing true happiness.

A sense of power and trust embodies us when we know clearly what we need and pursue that consistently and with faith — faith that God or Our Creator invites us to feel satisfied. After all, when we are gratified, we are in the best position to fulfill our role in the universe and help others do the same.

EXERCISE 10 — *Your Schedule*

Reflect on your daily schedule. Note the times of day when you are most energized. How do you feel first thing in the morning? 10 a.m.? noon? 2 p.m.? 4 p.m.? 6 p.m. and 8 at night? During the day, do you sense an urge to nap or rest?

Note your eating habits. When do you eat meals and when do you snack? Do you use meals to provide your body with energy? Do you eat when you are hungry or when the clock says noon?

Note times when you seem to struggle. When do you feel lethargic? When do you use caffeine to counter fatigue? How else do you boost your energy? How else could you?

Do you rest during the day? When? How do you feel during these breaks? What happens when you do not rest? What happens when you eat on the run, when you are in an all-day meeting, when you travel in your car for long periods?

Now, consider:

- If you did not use an alarm clock, what time would you wake in the morning naturally?
- What activities do you like to do best in the morning? in the afternoon?
- What is the hardest time of day for you to concentrate and accomplish a task?
- What time would be the best for you to eat traditional meals?

A contented person knows who he is, what is essential to his life, and involves himself in activities to meet those requirements. You can be one of those people if you listen to the messages your mind, your heart, and your body give you. Try it. See how much more joy will come into your life!

EXERCISE 11 — Your Likes and Dislikes

List who you are right now — the roles you play in your life. Include roles like daughter, son, father, mother, employee, employer, carpenter, executive. Also, list your basic characteristics — are you a caring person, a fighter, sensual, aggressive, fun, outgoing? Write as many characteristics as you can.

Now, what do you enjoy in life? If you were a millionaire, how would you spend your time? Consider activities you do not enjoy that you "have" to do. List those.

As you live the next few days, become aware of what you do each day that brings you joy. Keep a running list of tasks you like. As you try new activities, note whether you enjoy them or not.

How often do you do things in your life you really enjoy? What do you do instead?

5

STEP 5
REALIGN YOUR COMMITMENTS TO SUIT YOUR NEEDS

In Step 4, we discovered an essential component of our happiness process — acknowledging and esteeming our needs. We now see the significance of need gratification. If we have been hiding our true self, we have uncovered it. If we have not listened to our true self, we know now that it calls us to action, and we can hear it doing so if we pay careful attention.

The next step in our Happiness Model is to align our commitments to suit our needs. What we do in life must fulfill our basic requirements if we are to realize true joy. To be happy, our needs and our commitments must coincide.

Life is an active process — it is doing all the things we do each day. It is traveling to work, reading to our children, taking an afternoon nap, sitting in traffic, folding laundry, bathing in the sun, calling a friend, and singing in church. Even when we are "being" rather than "doing," we are still doing since we are breathing, relaxing, playing, concentrating, praying, or meditating.

What we do either satisfies our needs or does not. What we do makes us happy or does not. Evaluating what you do and its effect on your joy is the next crucial step in our happiness process.

What is a Commitment?

A commitment is an activity, a matter, or an event we have pledged to undertake, address, accomplish, or attend. A commitment can involve a job, another person (such as a marriage), a child, or a volunteer activity. We commit ourselves mutually to friends and family members.

Our commitments may be with other people, ourselves, or with an institution, like a company or nonprofit organization. We can solidify a commitment verbally or in writing, such as through a legally-binding contract. Other commitments are simply understood, like the commitment to a friendship.

Commitments are important, because commitments are what we do. If we are committed to complete a task, we spend time in our life — maybe every day of our lives — working on that task. If we are committed to a relationship, we all know that relationships take time. We talk with that person, meet for lunch, go to a movie, help them with a problem, socialize with them.

Areas to examine while reflecting on your commitments include:

- your partner
- your family
- your time
- your job
- your children
- your community
- your home
- your financial commitments
- your friends
- your place of worship

When we look at commitments and needs side by side, we begin to see agreements and tasks that fit our life, and those that do not. The commitments that make sense gratify you and make you feel alive. When working on that commitment, we realize joy.

Other duties, however, cause us stress. We don't feel right about the commitment, or we are not happy fulfilling it. Or, we force ourselves to fulfill the agreement and cause ourselves heartache.

When a commitment does not answer your essential self, when you sense a disconnect, you face a crucial decision. Do you continue doing it (ignoring your needs) or do you make a change? If you decide to make a change, do you revise the promise or eliminate it completely?

These are your choices and your decisions. One path — staying with a commitment that does not make you happy — will hold you in a position of frustration and discontent. You will have little time or energy left to satisfy your true self.

If your job is stressful, you might not feel up to calling friends once you get home. You might resist a creative activity like painting because you lack the strength. You might miss interacting with your children, going for a walk, playing a game, or talking with your mate. Instead, you might choose to sit in front of television to unwind.

The other choice — altering our commitments — opens us up to pleasure. It releases your soul, exposing the possibility of hearing and addressing your inner self. Without the drain of agreements which take away from our joy, we have more time and energy to spend gratifying our essential desires. We hear our desires more clearly because our mind is more settled.

Let's look at an example. One of the biggest agreements each of us makes is to a lifelong partner or companion. Whether a heterosexual or homosexual relationship, a marriage or a live-in partner — a commitment to another person is a serious matter.

Review your relationship with your lifelong partner if you have one. Verify that the relationship is what you truly desire. Does the relationship fulfill you? Does it lift you up or bring you down? Energize you or demoralize you? Are you truly committed to this relationship or making a half-hearted effort? Important to you at one time, is this partnership still a priority?

You might answer that yes — you are still committed to this relationship and it does, in fact, satisfy your needs. Great. Keep doing what you are doing. Keep seeing joy.

If, however, the partnership does not satisfy your needs, you have a number of options. You can spend time working on the relationship, seeking outside counsel to improve it. You can communicate your discontent or revise your expectations. You can rebuild the commitment from the ground up.

Acknowledging that the commitment no longer satisfies you will open you to the possibility of joy. You then have a choice to revise your pledge, work on improving it, or eliminate it.

Why We do What we Do

If you have changes to make in your life, you might ask: How did I get into this mess? How did my life get this far off course? How did I commit myself to so much that does not fulfill my basic needs?

The answers are complex. For some, as we discussed in Step 4, we were never taught to listen to our inner self. Our commitments were based on what we felt we should or must do. Our commitments were made because we felt obligated to serve another person above ourselves. Our commitments were made with no thought about how they would impact our happiness.

For others, we have known change is necessary, but we have been scared. It takes courage to change, and you might not have been ready.

Obligations and apprehension about change might have caused us to stay in the same job or with the same person long after these commitments seemed no longer appropriate. We might be living in the same area, keeping the same friends, attending the same church, even though our desires are not being met.

Whatever the reason, change is eminent now. We know that to be happy, we must align our commitments with our essential needs in mind. If we choose not to do so, we choose sorrow. If we choose to do so, we choose joy.

How do we go about changing our commitments to suit us? First, we must eliminate obligations — musts and shoulds — from our life. We must learn to say no when obligations do not address our true needs. We must learn not to overcommit. And, we must learn to recognize when an opportunity to satisfy comes our way.

These might seem daunting tasks, but they are worthwhile and necessary in our pursuit of joy.

Eliminating Obligations

We must remove obligations — disguised as musts and shoulds — from our life to make room for joy. Many of us live as we feel obligated to do so. Musts and shoulds dictate how we act, what we do, and with whom we interact.

We all are born knowing exactly what we need. When hungry, we cry. When needing to dispose of waste from our body, we do so. When in fear, we stop or reach out. When needing to play, we pick up a toy. When needing to explore, we open a cabinet.

Watch a toddler's determination to engage in activities she enjoys, moment to moment. At 26 months, my daughter went through a stage where every item she requested she "needed." Rather than saying "I want," she would say: "I need juice." "I need my dolly." "I need you to talk." "I need cracker." How refreshing to hear a toddler speak!

As children grow, however, parents, teachers, friends, and society often send them "should" messages. I hear parents say: "You shouldn't do" this, "You shouldn't do" that. "We don't do" this, "We don't do" that. These rules stick in our minds and even when situations change, or we change, our minds still reiterate that "should."

Society as a whole feeds us should messages:

- I should be in great shape.
- I should have a shiny car.

- I should have an immaculate house.
- I should worship.
- I should spend time with my children.
- I should exercise every day or three times per week.
- I should buy soap or detergent or cosmetics or stylish clothes.
- I should take my car for an oil change every 3,000 miles.
- I should drink eight glasses of water per day.

By the time we live up to all the shoulds in our life, we have little time left to do for ourselves! Should we do or be all these things? If so, will we be happy?

The Case of Tom

Tom has struggled with his weight his entire life. At 5'10", he weighs 250 pounds. Society would say he is overweight. More important, he feels overweight and uncomfortable. At 32 years of age, Tom has been chronically overweight since age 14.

Part of Tom's weight problem stems from messages he received from his parents, mainly his father. A chef, Tom's father owns a catering business and prides himself on food preparation, presentation, and taste. The family patriarch, he cooks every holiday and practically every evening. He uses the freshest ingredients, real butter, whole milk, white flour, and rich sauces. He bakes lavish desserts.

When alone in his own home, Tom seems to eat well. He keeps fresh vegetables and fruits in the house, and he limits his intake of fat and sugar. But, when he visits his parents, he cannot curb his appetite. He often eats uncontrollably, reverting to his childhood days when he ate and ate but was active enough to burn off the calories. The problem is he visits his parents twice a week!

As a medical assistant, Tom has a high-stress job and often eats on the run. Then, he stops for fast food on his way home. A health care professional, Tom is embarrassed among his colleagues. He knows being overweight is unhealthy, and years of obesity are beginning to take their toll. He lacks energy and loses breath while walking up stairs.

Is Tom happy following in his parents' footsteps — eating rich foods and keeping excess fat in his diet? Would he be happier thinner? Would he be happier healthier?

If Tom looked closely at his personal needs, he might discover that he would be happier — not necessarily thinner — but certainly healthier. Taking charge of his body, eating healthily, and exercising might help Tom see his true self and greater joy.

Reflect on the messages about food you might have received as a child. In my house, my mother told us to "finish everything on the plate." Even when I was full, I was told I should finish my meal.

Another rule: "You can't have cake until you finish the rest of your meal." When deprived of sweets, we often use cake, candy, and ice cream as a source of power and control, rather than food for energy. To feel powerful, in control, or worthy, we might overeat or indulge in sweets or fatty foods.

Even the satisfaction of a basic need, like food, carries messages from the past. To satisfy our need for food, do we have to overeat? Do we have to eat unhealthily? Do we have to hurt our bodies?

Here's another example of how messages can harm our inner-self. About four years ago, I decided to work part-time. I was moderately happy in my job, but my real passion was writing.

I reduced my hours to part-time and spent the extra 20 hours a week writing. I attended a screen writing class and worked diligently on a script, drafting 250 pages. It was good, and I was pleased with myself.

Then, I got stuck. I had written a wonderful beginning, developed solid characters, devised an exciting plot, and mastered a gripping conflict. Drafting the climax, however, paralyzed me.

I fell into a moderate depression for some time over this. I put the screenplay away and worked on other projects. I went back to the script — wrote a few more scenes here and there — but I never finished it. It still sits in my desk drawer.

Ruminating the shoulds in my life made me even more disillusioned over this project. In my mind, I kept repeating to myself: "When you start a project, you should finish it."

I knew I should finish the screenplay. After all, look what I had sacrificed to write it? A good job. All that time in front of the computer! Besides, I was so close. If I could just finish it! I would be rich — maybe famous! And happy?

Years later — that screenplay is still sitting in my desk incomplete. I dream of finishing it one day. I still might sell it one day. But, for now, other projects occupy my mind. Should I finish it? No. Do I want to finish it? Maybe. Must I finish it? No way! Do I need to finish it. Perhaps. But, these are my decisions to make, no one elses!

My advice: remove the world *SHOULD* from your vocabulary

completely. Should is a hurtful word that introduces us to guilt, inadequacy, sadness, and low self-esteem.

If you find yourself saying "should," replace the word with "could," "I want to," or "it would be nice if." Then, see how you respond to this new statement. If you still want to do the action, by all means, do it. Realize you have an option.

Another way to readjust the shoulds and musts in your life is to ask yourself: What will happen if I do not do this? What would happen if I were sick and *could* not do this?

Remember — shoulds are usually someone's opinion, or a ploy to make us buy products. Companies plant shoulds in our mind to convince us we need their product. Parents plant shoulds in our mind so we act a certain way. These shoulds may have been appropriate for us as a child. But, we are different now. We are adults, with new circumstances, new skills, and different viewpoints on need fulfillment.

EXERCISE 12 — Reviewing Musts and Shoulds

First thing tomorrow, write down all the activities you would like to accomplish that day.

Now, put an "M" next to the activities you MUST achieve and an "S" next to the activities you SHOULD do. Identify the items you NEED to work on with an "N," and those you WANT to achieve with a "W."

Promise yourself that you will accomplish all the items you NEED to do first. Then, put your list away. Go about your day and try to live in the present.

At the end of day, answer the following questions:
- How many items on your list did you accomplish?
- Did you accomplish the items you most NEEDED to do? most WANTED to do?
- Did you really have to work on all the items you labeled a MUST? What happened if you did not?
- Did you accomplish any of the items labeled SHOULD? Who is telling you you SHOULD finish these tasks?

Someone from your past may have planted should messages in your mind. Now, as an adult, the person telling you you should or must do a task is you! Your shoulds and musts are now self-inflicted. Acceptance now is voluntary.

Our job as adults, with a mind of our own, is to listen to messages we received in the past, assess our unique position, then decide whether to adopt or abandon the message. This applies to the messages we hear now as well.

If the advice makes sense — go for it. If not, don't do it. Even if it does make sense, we might not be ready to hear it. We might choose to find our own way or consult yet another person. Whatever the decision, the choice is yours.

Besides eliminating obligations, another great step in realigning our commitments is to learn to say no. Often, we agree to something before we have thought it through completely. Our initial instinct is to please — please someone else before ourselves. So, we say yes — of course we will do it!

Then, reality sets in. We realize afterwards the mess we have caused. We might have to sacrifice our free time to do this deed. We might have to inconvenience our family or ourselves.

Always consider your needs before making a promise. Learn to distinguish when a favor helps you feel more worthwhile and happier — or puts more pressure on your life and brings you down.

Overcommiting — not being able to say no — is a clear barrier to happiness. People often accept too many commitments, doing for others above themselves. Then, the matters that deserve their greatest attention — those that make them the happiest — fall to the side while they do for others.

Look how many activities and relationships you have in your life. Physically and emotionally, you might not be able to do it all. If you continue this pace, your true self will suffer. Your desires will not be met, and you will forgo happiness.

Where are you on your priority list? Where do your needs fit in on your list of things to do?

Think carefully before you make a promise. If someone asks you a favor or offers you an opportunity — take time to review your options thoroughly. If the person insists on an answer immediately, say no. It is better to let an opportunity pass then make a rash decision based on pressure.

I'm not advocating selfishness. If your desires are met, and you have extra time, by all means, take on more or volunteer to assist others. I'm suggesting, however, that your wishes are significant, too. If you are not happy, your time might be better spent centering on yourself a while.

The Courage to Change

The process of creating more happiness in your life will likely include eliminating or revising commitments that no longer gratify you. It will mean saying no to people. It will mean retracting on pledges you have made.

When I first began to eliminate or revise commitments in my life, the one area which required grave attention was my friendships. I was everybody's friend. I prided myself on lifelong friendships. I was a friend any friend would love to have because my friends came first. My friends came before myself.

When I examined some of my friendship with a new focus — a focus on my joy — I recognized that some were no longer appropriate. Perhaps we had lost touch, or I was giving more to the friendship than I was receiving in return. Some friendships had become geographically undesirable — the people lived too far away, so seeing each other regularly was difficult. It had become a chore rather than a joy.

In one case, I was maintaining a friendship with someone who constantly complained about his situation but was unwilling to make concrete progressions toward solutions. When we spoke, his complaints brought me down. His downtroddened spirit was starting to depress me! The friendship was tedious.

After careful examination, I chose to remove that friendship from my life. Instead, I pledged to spend my time developing and maintaining joyful relationships.

This confrontation took courage. I was afraid to discuss my decision with my friend, but I did so honestly. I was not critical but I was clear. After the conversation, I felt relieved.

When revising or eliminating a commitment, be honest, clear, and courteous with the other person involved. Carefully explain your new outlook. Speak about what you know to be true for you today and note that your situation may change tomorrow.

If you want to alter a commitment, be clear about your limitations. If the other person expects too much from you, set the boundaries. Be open to negotiation and flexible but keep your needs at the forefront of discussion.

Some commitments you will want to eliminate promptly and abruptly. You might choose to ease out of others, preparing you and the other person or institution involved. A change in careers, for example, might take time. You might need to get finances together or seek counsel for alternatives. You might need to warn your supervisors of your pending decision, preparing them to hire someone else to take your place. You might propose to finish a job you are in the midst of, then tell the person you cannot recommit. Or, you might mention that this may be your last commitment to them. You might find another person who can fulfill the commitment, though you cannot.

Know you are entitled to change your mind! Agreements make sense when we make them. Later, situations change. You have the right to revisit a promise and eliminate or revise it.

I encourage you to "clean house" in your commitments. You might find that you choose your agreements more carefully. You might say "no" more easily. You might find that making a clear, concise, and thoughtful commitment to a job, a person, or a community an invigorating experience.

I remember when I first began to commit based on my inner-self. It was such a strange sensation. It took me three years to eliminate all the commitments in my life that did not gratify me. I eliminated my job and some of my relationships. I abandoned many messages I received as a child.

My only commitments at that point were to my husband, my children, my home, my family, and a few friends. I sat in that state of relative non-commitment for some time, reaffirming that letting go of the past was right for me. I was scared, yet determined to   live my life in keeping with my true self.

After grieving the loss of precious time, I began to build strength. I started to fill my life with activities that were true to me. I agreed to tasks based on instinct and faith, trying not to direct the outcome. I had confidence that if I acted on instinct, I could handle any situation I faced.

I started doing activities I enjoyed — exercising, hiking, relaxing, writing, painting, calling and being with friends, spending quality time with my husband and family. I started doing activities I always intended to do, but was too busy or too fearful to try.

My confidence in acknowledging my needs and following my heart increased and strengthened. Soon, acting on the self became easy and natural. I was and am happier than I have ever been in my life, living this way.

Realigning your commitments will change your life. You may find more time to involve yourself in activities that please you. You may find more time to be with people who fill you with joy. You may find yourself making conscious promises — promises

EXERCISE 13 — Rethinking Your Commitments

In Exercise 5, you listed some of your commitments. Take time now to review and evaluate them. Did you forget any? Don't forget promises you have made to yourself. What specifically are the tasks and activities you perform because of your commitments? What specifically have you agreed to accomplish? When did you make these commitments? How did you make them?

Note the people to whom you are committed. How are you connected? How deep are these commitments, and how do they feel to you?

Consider the following:

- Which commitments are most stressful or make you most anxious? Why?
- Which commitments fulfill a basic need? Which need?
- Which tasks and activities make you truly happy? Most happy?
- Which commitments seem appropriate to you?
- Which do you most want to eliminate? Why haven't you done so to date?
- Is there anyone on your list to whom you would like to talk about your commitments? If so, who and what would you say?

made intentionally to fulfill your desires.

When we live with an eye on our desires, the world transforms to a different place — it seems to line up to support us. It seems to lift us to be our best. After all, the world invites us to be ourselves since we have a unique and special place in it. When we find that true and special place, the world applauds. Natural order is restored. Opportunities open in incredible and unexpected ways.

True adulthood and freedom comes when we act on our instincts, fearlessly, with divine trust. True adulthood and freedom comes when we recognize that we are important in our lives — as important as anyone or anything else. True adulthood and freedom comes when we choose to love and please ourselves.

When we are true to ourselves, we are also true to God or The Creator who made us unique and able to contribute sincerely to society. Through knowing and loving ourselves, we can be happy and ready to serve the world.

Know who you are, honor who you are, and incorporate who you are into your everyday commitments. What a pleasure when your activities and needs match. What a release when your tasks, your work, and your relationships coincide with your essential self. What energy! What happiness!

Then, your true self is alive!

STEP 6
LIVE IN THE PRESENT

Steps 1 through 5 of our Happiness Model addressed the importance of making happiness our number one priority, taking control of our lives, and honoring others and the world as they are. We also acknowledged the significance of understanding and fulfilling our fundamental needs.

One characteristic of happiness is essential for us to acknowledge now. Knowing and incorporating the concept into our lives will aid our journey to increased joy. Before we can be happy, we must realize that happiness occurs here and now — in the present. Happiness is today, and we must be present to what we are doing to experience joy.

Author Mihaly Csikszentmihalyi calls being present "flow." In *Finding Flow, The Psychology of Engagement in Everyday Life*, Csikszentmihalyi defines "flow" as being fully focused and immersed in what you are doing at the time you are doing it. In flow, a person considers intensely the matter at hand. He is not looking back or forward, not concentrating on any matter other than the one facing him.[17]

In flow, a person is challenged, but not overly taxed to the point of frustration.[18]

Say, for instance, you are at work. You arrive and have a meeting at 10 a.m. Between 8 and 10 a.m., your time is unstructured. You have not agreed to be anywhere at any given time. You are "free" to work on pending projects.

Some of your projects have tighter deadlines than others. Some work interests and challenges you more than others. One project frightens you. It is way over your head, and your boss expects your performance to be paramount. You feel anxious and worried about this particular project. You put that one on hold for a while.

Instead you take out another folder. You look at the progress you have made on this project and center your thoughts. You resist thinking about the other projects on your desk, particularly the one what concerns you most.

You are making progress on the project at hand. As time passes, you sense the need to call a client for information, and you do so. Then, you need research information in a computer file. You look it up. Later, you need the advice of a colleague down the hallway, so you walk down to talk to her.

Your work flows. You move along, accomplishing tasks, gathering information, progressing on the job. You don't even know it, but you are content. Soon, you look at your clock and realize it's 9:50 a.m. Your meeting is in 10 minutes! Time passed so quickly. You were in "flow." Now, the flow is broken.

Author John Baucom calls being present living "in the moment." In *Baby Steps to Happiness*, he recommends living one moment in time -- not "for" the moment, but "in the moment ... appreciating and savoring every moment of your life. It's experiencing intensely what you are doing, at the moment you are doing it ... block out extraneous thoughts and distractions and become absorbed in the present."[19]

Being present means living life as it occurs to us.[20] It means following our instincts — seeing and listening to the natural order of life and reacting to that order when it calls us into action.

Often, our mind is too preoccupied to really concentrate on what we are doing. Our mind is too busy to hear natural order calling us to action. Sometimes, we are thinking about the past or the future or thinking about how much we dislike the task at hand. We might be considering what another person did to us earlier in the day or dreaming about where we would rather be.

If, however, we really concentrate on exactly what we are doing when we are doing it, the amazing happens. Our mind centers. Our urges relax. Our body calms. Our heart feels content. We are now open to the flow experience and open to happiness.

Next time you engage in a task — particularly one you do not enjoy — focus on being happy. Be fully present to exactly what you are doing at the time — not where you are going, but where you are. Do not consider what you would rather be doing or dream about tomorrow. Center your energy on the experience that is now.

You might find that time passes rapidly. You might find your mind flowing. You might find living in the moment a joyous way to live.

Our current lifestyle challenges us to slow down and center ourselves. After all, many of us are juggling a career, a family, and a home. We are attempting to please not only ourselves, but our companion, our children, our parents, our siblings, and our friends. Our demands are high, and it seems we cannot keep up without doing two things at once.

A friend of mine said recently: "I need more time, not less. I need to speed up, not slow down. I can't focus on one thing. I have too much to do."

The Case of Debra

Debra lives her life with lists. As a single mom, Debra has a busy schedule, working full-time, taking care of two young children. She prides herself on being well-organized. She says, "I don't know how I would get through a day if I didn't keep myself organized!"

Each day — in her appointment book — Debra writes tasks she needs to complete that day. The list includes projects, errands, items to purchase, appointments, and calls to make. Some days, just looking at the list overwhelms Debra. She worries she might forget something or not accomplish all she has to do.

Recently, Debra started to plan weeks and months in advance. Goal-setting, she says, helps her stay focused. She now maintains a daily list of things to do, a weekly list, and lists for the week after that and the week after that.

Debra also creates lists so she won't forget important items — groceries, clothes she and her children need, and names and addresses of influential people. She takes note of places she would like to visit, job leads, items she wants for her home, even friends she would like to call.

Debra would like to live more for today, but she doesn't know how. She has so much to do, and she feels she must accomplish everything. After all, her kids depend on her, her boss depends on her. She cannot afford to jeopardize her children's future or her job. If she doesn't stay on top of what must to be done, she falls behind.

Is Debra living in the past, the future, or the present?

One day, I recommended to Debra that she throw out all her lists. Her eyes widened: "What? My lists? No way!" I had suggested the unimaginable.

We started small. I looked over Debra's daily "to do" list and suggested she continue to draft it. But, instead of having it in front of her Monday morning, I asked her to put it aside and really concentrate on her work that day. I asked her not to look at the list or consider it while managing her day.

To pacify her fear of forgetting an essential task, I suggested that she review the list about 3 p.m. to ensure she had not forgotten anything.

Debra reluctantly agreed. Monday came and went. That night, she called. Debra had experienced the most productive, yet relaxing day of work she ever had. The day just "flowed," she said. "Not only did I accomplish everything on my list — by 3 p.m., I was completely finished! I picked my children up early from day care, and they helped me make dinner!" I never heard her happier.

Working truly present — not looking at her structure or trying to control her day — Debra was free to listen to her instincts and life's natural order. Without worry about what she needed to accomplish or whether she would complete or forget a task, Debra was free to enjoy herself. She was open to flow.

In the hustle and bustle of today's society, being present to what you are doing (when you are doing it) is going to take practice. Distractions are all around us. The phone rings, our focus is broken. The kids fight, drawing our attention elsewhere. We hit an obstacle and frustration surfaces, clouding our view of the task at hand.

Here are some clear signals that we are not living in the moment:

- doing two things at once.
- thinking about what happened yesterday or last week. Dreaming about tomorrow or reaching a goal.
- thinking about being somewhere else.
- focusing on the fact that you do not like what you are doing.
- second-guessing your instincts when they occur to you. Listening to rationale, instead of your heart, your inner-spirit, or your intuition.
- being frustrated by an obstacle, rather than centered on overcoming it effectively and moving forward.

I'm a classic example of someone who lived life out of flow. I used to pride myself on managing two activities at once. I would watch television and cross stitch, talk to my husband and wash dishes, drive and feed my children crackers in the back seat. I would talk to a friend while opening the mail. I would lie down to rest and think about tomorrow.

I was focused on accomplishing too much too fast, trying to force life to go my way. Once I realized the world has a natural order and everything happens as it is meant to happen (when it is meant to happen), my hurried lifestyle seemed pointless. I realized that you cannot live present if you are trying to dictate tomorrow. You cannot live in the present if you are too busy to hear your internal messages.

Dwelling on the Past

Dwelling on the past — even a joyful past — takes away our ability to experience flow and, therefore, our ability to be happy. Remembering might foster a smile or sharpen our desire to meet with happiness again. But, the cost of thinking about yesterday is today. While reviewing yesterday, we miss now.

Reliving the past often makes us sad. When nostalgic, many people long for how life used to be. Remembering the "good old days," they wonder why the world has changed so drastically. I overheard a 72-year-old woman say recently, "I want things to be the way they used to be."

Other people do not long for the past, they wish they could alter it. Some people spend an enormous amount of time reliving their mistakes, wishing they could go backwards in time. Or, they might spend effort trying to prevent making the same mistake twice.

How often have we thought about calling a friend, then changed our mind? Maybe we were in the middle of a task at work, and a person we have not seen in a while came to mind. The phone was right there. Instead of picking it up, we thought: "They are probably busy. I will finish what I'm doing, then call."

Our mind — and the past — told us to ignore our instincts. Maybe we called that person a few months ago, and they told us how busy their life had become. Now, we think they might be too busy to spend 10 minutes talking to us.

Perhaps we were told to finish a project before moving onto the next. That message prevents us from interrupting what we are doing and calling our friend. It prevents us from acting on our instincts.

How dangerous to think that the past influences the present. How sad to miss out on today while thinking about yesterday. The past is just that — past. It can neither be changed nor relived, and it has little relevance to the life we choose to live now. Forget yesterday and start fresh today knowing that this instance is when real joy can and does occur.

The Uncertain Future

Like rehashing or reliving the past, dreaming too much about the future can prevent us from experiencing joy. Sad as it might seem, tomorrow might never come. If we spend our life dreaming about tomorrow (even a bright future), we miss the very moment that is today!

Some people spend an enormous amount of time fantasizing. They think: "Once I'm finished doing the laundry (or working, cleaning the house, driving the kids to school, watching this television show), I will be happy. Then, I can play golf (or go on vacation, or take a walk, or watch my favorite show)." They think once they have made a million dollars, taken their kids to college, solved a problem, or cured an illness, they will return to joy.

Some other common misconceptions are:

- I will be happy when my wife (or husband) gets her (or his) act together
- I will be happy after my father apologizes
- I will be happy when I buy my new home
- I will be happy when my kids don't whine so much
- I will be happy when this mood passes

The problem with forecasting is that happiness happens now — not in the future. If we are waiting for something to occur before we can be happy, that instance might never come. Or, it arrives, and it looks different than we expected or we start fulfilling another dream. Moreover, we waste the very moment that is now getting there.

My belief is that pondering the future is often our way of attempting to govern it. After all, if we focus on tomorrow, it might become what we envision. We might be able to second-guess it. We might be able to make it what we want. Perhaps our dreams will come true.

Fancying that you can rule the future is a mistake. You cannot control the future, and if you try to do so, you are going against the very core of being present — listening to your instincts and accepting natural order.

The world has natural order, and we have a position in that order. Our instincts call us to a specific position in that order. If we are too busy structuring our lives or directing our destiny, our hearts cannot listen to messages. Or, we ignore the message to maintain control.

Each of us can shape and mold our destiny. We can draft long and short-term goals to help us reach that future. When a voice calls us in another direction, however, it is important that we listen and consider acting. We might have a future in mind, but our soul might have another in our heart.

Don't miss today by trying to dominate the future. In trying to control, we miss the very instance that is now — and life itself.

Living Joyfully in the Present

I remember when I first started converging on the present, living each instance when it occurred to me. Before then, I seldom focused — truly focused — on any task while I was doing it.

I was a classic case of someone living for tomorrow. I thought I would find peace when I was rich or thin or when I married or when I had a big house or children. I would be happy when I left my job, followed my dream, wrote my book, took that dream vacation.

Motivated by achievement, I focused on one goal, then another. I had my eye on that golden apple and structured my life to reach that apple, convinced that the end result was going to make me happy.

In the meantime, though, I missed the pleasures of life that just bestow themselves to you, unplanned and unimagined. You cannot schedule time to smell the roses — the roses just appear to you, and your heart calls you to smell them. I was too busy to smell the roses. I seldom took time to rest or call a friend while working. I seldom took care of my needs when they called me to action.

When the idea of living in the present was given to me, I couldn't imagine living life that way. I could only remember once in my life being present to what I was doing. That was on my honeymoon, snorkeling in the Caribbean. I was alone in the water, my head just under the surface. I saw schools of fish below and felt I was swimming with them.

I was aware of my breathing. I heard the air going in and out of my body through the snorkeling tube. The sound was meditating and calming. I was not thinking about what was happening on the shore, where my husband was, or whether I was snorkeling correctly. I wasn't worried about getting bitten by a shark or barracuda. My mind was fully present, and my heart fully contented.

Remembering that incident made me realize how joyous living in the moment could be. I tried replicating that experience in my everyday life. I concentrated more and paid more attention to my body and my desires calling me to action.

When I was tired, I slept. When I was hungry, I ate. When I wanted to call a friend, I picked up the phone. When I wanted to work, I worked. When I wanted a break, I took a break. I did what occurred to me the instance it did.

What a change from my rigid, structured life! As I practiced being present, I noticed amazing results. Time seemed to stop. My whole life, whole world slowed down. I was more attentive during conversation. I felt myself understanding people more and having better one-on-one relationships. I felt like people were listening to me more, too.

I was more productive than ever. My work flowed naturally, and I felt less stress and pressure. I enjoyed the process of meeting my goals.

The best part of all: even with increased productivity, I found lots of time left over. I found time to read to my daughter and walk in the afternoon. I found time to cat nap and garden. I found time to put bird seed in my bird feeder.

The two areas of my life that were most impacted because of living in the moment were eating and resting. Before I began living this way, I seldom centered when eating. I would eat in my car or stand at the kitchen counter. I would pick at this morsel, pick at that. I would finish what my children left on their plates. I would go out with a friend and talk and talk, not realizing how much I was eating.

Now, I sharpen my attention every time I eat or drink. I read about nutrition. I plan meals and set aside time to prepare them. I sit with every item in front of me. I smell the food and taste each bite, savoring each morsel. I chew completely and take my time.

The results are profound. Not only did I lose weight, but I enjoy eating so much more now. I eat less, with more satisfaction. I even like the taste of water!

Similarly, my ability to rest has improved. Before, I would lie down and thoughts would race through my head. I would plan the future, rehash the past. My mind would not rest, so my body could not.

Now, through breathing, meditation, or other relaxation techniques, I calm my mind and my body. I put my head on a soft pillow, envelope my body with a comfortable, warm blanket. I curl up next to my husband and feel his body close to mine. I feel the sensation of relaxing all the way to my toes. It's like a wave overtaking me and calming my soul. Now, when I rest, I feel rejuvenated and refreshed because I truly rest.

We all can remember states of "non-flow" — times when we are so frazzled by the day's activities that we couldn't focus on anything or slow down to relax.

Perhaps you remember the intensity of such a state. Perhaps you were driving, not paying attention to the road. A small animal darts out in front of you. You turn the wheel, jerking your car across the center line, just missing an oncoming car. Your heart beats heavily, and you take a deep breath, realizing how close you came to a head-on collision.

Or, maybe you were talking to a friend on the phone when your children start arguing in an adjacent room. You try to focus, but your attention is on the kids. In the middle of a sentence, you interrupt your friend, "Hold on, please."

Without listening for a response, you put the phone aside, turn to the children, and demand they settle down. They do, and you return to the conversation. "Now, what were you saying?"

How dangerous it is to be driving and not paying attention to the road! How hurtful it is to be conversing and not focusing on what the other person is saying. How sad it is to be living life and not paying attention to what we are doing when we are doing it. What a loss of joy!

Take time now to concentrate on living life here and now. Even during your most boring tasks — like doing laundry, sitting in traffic, watching a boring baseball game, sitting through a tedious speech — focus on each movement and each instance.

If you loathe laundry, note the smell of freshly washed towels. Feel the softness of your favorite sweatshirt. Notice the potpourri of colors as you pile shirts in their basket.

Know that by doing laundry, you are fulfilling a basic need — the need for symmetry and order in your life. We cannot have order in our lives if we have a pile of dirty clothes sitting in our closet. We cannot feel good about ourselves unless we pay attention to personal hygiene.

No matter what you are doing, take in all the sights and smells of the moment. Do one task at a time. Listen to the other person when you converse — really listen. Notice the world and absorb the colors and beauty around you. Savor each experience to its fullest.

Do not force the world to operate according to your schedule. As Dr. Susan Jeffers states in *"Feel the Fear and Do It Anyway,"* everything in life happens in perfect time.[21] Every incident is meant to occur at the very time it does. The world and the universe have their own time schedule. Accept it. See how much more joyful your life can be living in the present.

EXERCISE 14 — Being Present

Consider a time in your life when you were in "flow"-- fully focused and immersed in what you were doing. Remember, some people can only identify one or two times in their life when they were living present.

Write down this exact experience as it occurred to you. Where were you? What made you concentrate? Did you realize you were completely focused? Were you relaxed? alert? happy?

Now, remember a time when you were talking with someone and doing another task simultaneously. Think of other times when you were participating in two or three activities at once. What were you doing? How did that feel? How productive were you?

Now, examine a time when you were talking with someone and that person was involved in another activity while listening to you. How did you feel? Did you feel understood? How could that person have paid more attention to you?

What would happen if you chose to live your life doing one thing at a time instead of two or more? What would happen if you took the time to really listen to a person with whom you were conversing? Would this make you anxious? What would you fear about this?

As you practice living each day in the moment, note what changes you see in your life.

7
STEP 7
TRANSCEND NEGATIVE EMOTIONS

Steps 7 and 8 of our Happiness Model address situations where we get stuck in either negativity or fear, and therefore cannot move forward to a place of joy.

Step 7 focuses our attention on negativity and offers us concrete ways to move through it promptly and adequately. Step 8 addresses the specific emotion of fear, which often holds us back from change or taking risks.

It is unrealistic to assume that a person could experience bliss every second of each day. After all, negative emotions are part of human composition. We all will encounter sorrow, fear, and loss in our lives. We will have incidents of anger, frustration, disappointment, worry, or guilt. Acknowledging and moving through these emotions keenly puts us back on our track of joy.

By labeling these emotions "negative," I am not implying they are "bad." All emotions have a place in our lives. But, some feelings lift us, energize us, keep us centered, and move us toward infinite happiness. Others bring us down, drain our energy, distract us from our real purpose, and diminish our joy.

Negative emotions are useful in our search for unlimited pleasure because they often signal that a part of us has been hurt and is unhealed. Negativity leads us to a wound. As we address that wound, face it, and heal it, we can again move toward a state of peace.

Sometimes negativity alerts us to a tender spot injured as a child. Sometimes it reminds us that we are allowing someone else to govern our life. It might signal that our expectations are too high or that we need to clarify them more clearly. Other bothersome emotions imply we are resisting life as it stands, rather than surrendering to it.

Although sometimes we might feel our emotions control us, the truth is that our emotions are in our mind, and we have the capacity to change our mind and confront negativity head on. Negative feelings are engineered by us, and they can be transcended by us.

Negativity shows up to us as:

Anger	Frustration	Resentment
Anxiety	Guilt	Sadness
Blame	Hatred	Self-Pity
Depression	Hopelessness	Shame
Disappointment	Hurt	Stress
Embarrassment	Jealousy	
Fear	Rage	

You can add endlessly to this list. Some emotions listed above are "higher order" emotions and some are "lower order." Higher order emotions are anger, sadness, fear, and sorrow. Other emotions, such as rage, hatred, disappointment, jealousy, are lower order emotions. They are forms of anger, sadness, fear, and sorrow.

We experience anger over something that happened to us in the past and sadness when something did not happen. We fear what we imagine could happen, and we become sorrowful over something that cannot happen.[22]

Emotions can be confusing, and it is often difficult for us to comprehend exactly what we feel. More times than not, our feelings are intertwined. We feel hopeless, sad, stressed, angered, and frustrated all at once.

Let's look at each emotion listed above more closely. Some more common negative emotions are described in detail on the next few pages. Read these descriptions carefully and begin to clarify exactly what you feel. Clarify where you are getting stuck — is it anger toward others, disappointment in yourself, doubt about your abilities, or blaming others for your troubles? Do you see a pattern to your negativity?

Anger, Hatred, Jealousy, Rage, and Resentment

Anger is extreme displeasure with yourself, another person, or life. Anger signals that you feel hurt that something did not happen that you wanted to have happen. Someone or something did not live up to your expectations. You have disappointed yourself, or another person has hurt you. You could also be mad at the world for not doing what you intended, or not acting the way you wanted it to act.

Anger surfaces especially when you sense a trust has been broken. When angry, you feel someone or the world has treated you unfairly or without respect. Either you failed yourself, another person failed you, or the world failed you. You feel betrayed.

A person might become angry and jealous, thinking life has

been unfair to him, compared to others. He resents others who have more than he and experiences jealousy. This resentment and jealousy can lead to anger — even hatred. When someone says, "that person did not deserve that promotion," resentment and jealousy are showing their evil eye.

Repressed, anger builds and can lead to rage. When we ignore anger, we might find ourselves releasing it inappropriately. How often do we hear of a woman who has had a hard day at work. She comes home and takes that anger out on her husband and children. She has displaced anger and is expressing it inappropriately.

Sadness, Hurt, Depression, Hopelessness, and Disappointment

Sadness and depression occur when we feel bad that something did not happen. Sadness and depression are similar, although depression is a deep sadness we cannot seem to overcome. When hurt, hopeless, or disappointed, sadness or depression come to pass.

Sadness is a state of being grief stricken or intensely disappointed in ourselves, someone else, or life in general. We grieve what did not happen and wish for a different outcome. Sadness often brings tears and woe.

Depression can be mild, moderate, or chronic and can last weeks, months or years. Many depressed people show signs of inactivity — they are tired, listless, and cannot motivate themselves to accomplish even the most simple task, such as taking a shower. They might cry easily, become irritable, and think in extremes.

A seriously depressed person may contemplate suicide. Often, this feeling subsides with time. If you are depressed to the point of hurting yourself, talk to someone and work through the problem. Usually the feeling does not persist.

Considered a physical illness by some mental health professionals, depression might be triggered by low levels of Serotonin — a chemical — in the body. I read once that the average woman faces four bouts of depression in her lifetime. That is the number reported! Most experts theorize that depression occurs equally as often in men. Women, however, seek treatment in greater numbers.

Depression often manifests in the presence of deep and sorrowful loss — such as the loss of a loved one or a job. Both sadness and depression signal that a person has sustained a loss he needs to address and mourn. The loss is sometimes recognizable, but sometimes not, such as loss of innocence, self-esteem, value, or purpose. The loss often reminds the person of a former loss he never resolved.

Fear, Anxiety, Tension, Stress, and Worry
Fear occurs when we worry about the future. We cannot control the future, and we anticipate that something we want to happen is not going to happen. We anticipate the worst.

Step 8 of our book will examine the special emotion of fear and address ways to overcome it. For now, however, know that fear is an unpleasant feeling we get when we anticipate danger on the horizon.

Stress and anxiety are the physical manifestation of fear, characterized by sweaty palms, a rapid heart rate, irritability, shaking, or a sick stomach. Tension is fear that paralyzes us into inaction. Worry is chronic anticipation of danger.

Frustration
Frustration arises when a person tries and tries but still fails. We become frustrated when we work vigorously and persistently on a problem, and it remains unsolved. Frustration arises when a situation does not occur as we expected, making us disappointed, dissatisfied, discouraged. These feelings then can lead to anger or sadness.

We encounter frustration when the world or others act differently than how we proposed they would act. Frustration is a signal that we are not honoring life as it stands or we are not honoring the way others act. We are frustrated life didn't go our way.

Frustration causes us to tense up as we fight reality. When frustrated, we center on how we WANT life to be or how we WANT people to act, rather than how they truly are.

Embarrassment, Shame and Unworthiness
Embarrassment, shame, and unworthiness are very destructive emotions, since they are projected onto ourselves. These emotions are inspired by feelings of guilt, shortcoming, impropriety, or regret. A person is embarrassed or shameful when he has disgraced or brought dishonor to himself. He feels unworthy of joy or honor, and these emotions can lead to intense sadness.

Embarrassment, shame, and unworthiness lead a person to hide or deny parts of themselves — the part they feel others will judge negatively. As we hide part of ourselves, we experience low self-esteem — believing a group or another person is better than us.

Some people become embarrassed or shameful or feel unworthy of respect and dignity because of a perceived weakness. Making mistakes in front of others or seeing others as free from error might inspire these sentiments.

Guilt, Blame, and Self-pity

While fear, anxiety, tension, and worry divert our attention to the future — guilt, blame and self-pity distract us to the past. When guilty, we feel bad about something we did. We made an error, a misjudgment, we sinned, or misbehaved, and we regret our actions.

Blame also transports us to the past, but we focus on what someone else did to injure us. We hold them responsible and accountable for our state of being, and this feeling often leads to anger toward that person.

In self-pity, we feel sorry for ourselves to the point of self-indulgence. Our sorrow lingers as we contemplate our misfortune. We cannot let go of the past and the hurts. Instead, we keep ruminating how horribly another person or the world treated us.

When experiencing guilt, blame or self-pity, we condemn ourselves, others, or the world for an impropriety. We punish ourselves, others, or the world for not acting the way we wanted them to act.

EXERCISE 15 — Pinpointing Negativity

The next time you feel uneasy, write down exactly what you feel. Pinpoint the exact emotion — anger, frustration, sadness, fear, etc. List every emotion that applies.

Now, examine if the emotion is directed at you, another person, or the world. Note who or what is involved.

Ask yourself the following questions:

- Are your emotions intertwined?
- How have you been dealing with negativity up to this point? What else could you do?
- Can you define a fear underlying the negative emotions you are experiencing? What is it?
- What would happen if you transcended these emotions as soon as possible?
- As long as you feel these emotions, can you be happy?
- The next time you are angry, sad, frustrated, worried, etc., what are you going to do?

Dealing with Negativity

Our goal now is to take our negativity — something we all feel at some time or another — and deal with it. We want to overcome negativity, move through it poignantly, and return to a state of joy.

Ignoring bothersome feelings can be a mistake. Often, we cannot justify our emotions, or we don't know how to react, so we push them aside. This is counterproductive. The first step in transcending our emotions is acknowledging them as real. If we chose to ignore them, negative emotions do not go away. Instead, we bury them in our psyche only to have them return later.

First, then, acknowledge the negativity. Clarify, using the descriptions in this section, exactly what you feel. Then, to surpass the emotion, act or think differently. Our active participation in confronting the emotion — by changing our actions or thought patterns — will help us return to joy.

Let's start with thinking differently. If we were to live our lives as outlined in the Happiness Model, some of our negativity would automatically subside. Downtrodden feelings would not surface to begin with because we would be spearheading our life, accepting it, living without judgment, and living in the moment. Living our Happiness Model can eliminate negativity before it even starts.

In Step 2, our model tells us to accept our life as it exists and take responsibility for it. In doing so, frustration decreases because we surrender to reality. We understand that we created our life, and we can recreate it. Why be frustrated under those conditions?

If we take charge of our lives, blame subsides since we cannot condemn others for our misfortunes if we govern our decisions. It is difficult, too, to be hurt or overcome by anger, resentment, hatred, or rage when we are taking care of our own lives. With no one else responsible for our happiness, how can someone else harm us? Why would we resent others? Where would we have room for hatred or hopelessness?

By incorporating Step 3 into our life — honoring others and the world without judgment — we can counter frustration and disappointment. If we see people as they are, there is little room for frustration and disappointment since these emotions arise when we don't surrender to reality as it exists. If we live accepting life the way it occurs to us, disappointment diminishes.

Eliminating judgment, too, can ease our frustration — and our resentment, anger, and sadness. Often, these sentiments surface because we feel "wronged" by another or the world. We were treated "unfairly," so we become frustrated, resentful, upset or saddened. By taking away judgment and accepting reality, these bothersome emotions become less prominent.

Steps 4 and 5 of our Happiness Model teach us to understand, acknowledge and fulfill our needs. With our requirements met, self-pity or jealousy have little room to germinate. We cannot pity ourselves if our needs are fulfilled. We cannot be jealous of others if our needs are met.

Taking care of ourselves implies we are worthy of respect. Our feelings of unworthiness diminish, and we are less wanting and less stressed.

Step 6 — living in the present — helps us release negativity. By centering on the present, we can counter anger, depression, guilt, or sadness. These emotions are all based on something someone did to us or did not do for us in the past. They are all past-focused, as is shame. We can confront fear, worry, anxiety, and tension by taking our mind off the horizon and living for now. With no anticipation, good or bad, we eliminate our source of concern, and with it, negativity.

You can see that changing our thought patterns — and changing how we live our life — can greatly improve our ability to eliminate negativity even before it surfaces.

When overtaken with negativity, think about how you can take control. Consider honoring the world and others for how it is and who they are. Reflect on your needs and how you can fulfill them. Converge on the present. Take charge of your life.

Actively Moving through Negativity

Sometimes changing how we think cannot remove our negative state. Sometimes, we must take additional action to transcend negativity. Sometimes we have to live through and experience the emotions we feel to transcend them.

In *Men are From Mars, Women are From Venus*, Dr. John Gray offers a helpful process for releasing negativity and returning to a loving — and therefore happier — state. Gray recommends writing down or journaling your feelings to express them and move through them.

He recommends writing a letter to the person at whom you feel angry, disappointed, or frustrated. You can also write this letter to yourself or to God — if the world has angered, disappointed, or frustrated you.

In your letter, state why you feel the way you feel, what saddens you about the situation, what you fear, and what you regret.

Then, express love.[23] Finally, pretend you are the other person and write a response letter to help you heal the pain.
Gray's model helps in several ways:

- You identify the emotion you feel
- You acknowledge the loss you feel
- You see the fear underlying the emotion
- You take responsibility by addressing what you regret
- You heal by expressing love and responding to yourself and your needs
- You transcend the emotion through the process

Let's look at how this process can help a person facing frustration.

The Case of Evelyn

Evelyn was frustrated by her job. She had been with the same company for 15 years, performing over and above her duties. Her supervisors had consistently rated Evelyn's performance as exceptional, and she had a reputation for getting the job done timely and efficiently.

This morning Evelyn found out a colleague — someone that she feels performs less than she — received a major promotion. This person is now going to be a vice president, in charge of one of the company's fastest-growing departments. Instead of being happy for him, Evelyn is frustrated, angry, and resentful. SHE deserved that promotion! Overwhelmed, Evelyn could not stop thinking about how this person's promotion reflected on her. She could not focus on her work. She talked with colleagues about the pain she felt. She was angry and disappointed in herself and the company.

Let's put Gray's model to work on Evelyn's problem.

Why is Evelyn frustrated, angry, resentful?
Evelyn is frustrated and angry because someone else was chosen for a promotion over her. She is resentful because this person did not work as hard as she but is still receiving rewards. She is frustrated because she has worked hard and is not receiving the benefits.

Why is Evelyn sad?
She is sad because she deserved that promotion. She
worked hard and deserved the reward.

What is Evelyn afraid of?
Evelyn is afraid that she will continue to work hard, and no
one will recognize her.   She is afraid no one notices her
now. She is afraid people will always pass her by.

What does Evelyn regret?
Evelyn regrets not being excited for this other person. She
regrets that she holds this anger.   She regrets that she
cannot express her frustrations to her boss.

Can Evelyn find love in the situation?
Evelyn works hard — for herself — not for anyone else.
She works hard to gratify her own needs of caring, dedica-
tion, and achievement. She is happy that her colleague got
a promotion. Good for him! To take more control of the
situation, Evelyn could express her desire for advancement
to her boss. Next time, he might consider her for promo-
tions if she shows an interest.

If Evelyn were to send a letter to the person who betrayed
her, what might this person say back to her?
The person could apologize for not recognizing more of
Evelyn's accomplishments. This person could explain her
actions – why the other person received the promotion. This
person could assure Evelyn that her work is appreciated and
recognized by her peers and supervisors. This person could
help Evelyn work on a plan to move her career forward.

Like all of us, Evelyn has unique feelings and a unique past
which influences how she feels. If you were going through the same
situation, you might not harbor the same feelings. You might, for
example, feel embarrassed that you were not promoted. You might
harbor anger toward yourself for not doing the best work possible.
You might regret not having taken charge of your career advancement.

Gray has filled his book with examples of how to use this tech-
nique to address an array of emotions. Practice this procedure to help
you face your negativity and transcend it. If you experience several
feelings at once, apply Gray's model to each separately. Write first
about your anger, then your frustration, then your guilt, and so on.

A few points to remember: Negativity often is rooted in a wound (and a fear) we received in childhood or early adolescence. If we heal the wound, our negativity lifts and often disappears. Until you completely heal the wound, negativity keeps coming back to remind you that the injury still exists. The faster you address the injury, the more rapidly you overcome the negativity.

Gray's model includes a section on fear to help us face these wounds. Often, we manifest anger, resentment, frustration, or depression in defense of our fear. Once we have faced what we dread, negativity ceases with it. In Step 8, we will address the special emotion of fear and ways to overcome it.

Other Ways to Overcome Negativity

If changing your thought patterns does not seem to address your negativity, nor does working through your pain by using Gray's model, you might want to try other techniques.

Some other techniques to move through bothersome feelings include:

- If your anger involves another person, express your anger to the person involved. A conversation often opens both hearts to understanding, intimacy, and healing. The other person might not realize she hurt you. She might apologize, moving you to closure. Do not express your anger to someone other than the person involved. Doing so seldom helps your anger dissipate.

- When sad, reflect on what you lost in the situation since sadness and depression originate with loss. Often, once we mourn the loss, the sadness disappears. Consider how this loss relates to other losses in your life. Mourn how you see fit to mourn — cry, take a long sad walk, watch the rain, spend a day in bed.

- Author Michael D. Yapko has studied people with depression, and sees a pattern in their behavior. To ease depression, he recommends setting short-term, middle, and long-term goals for yourself; controlling impulses; and seeing prospects as hopeful rather than hopeless.[24] He also advises seeing ambiguity in situations rather than experiencing life as black and white.[25] Association also can help ease depression. Force yourself to get out of the house. Call or visit friends regularly.

- If looking within or reaching out to friends does not seem to lift your sadness, consider seeking counsel from your doctor or a trained, licensed mental health professional. Depression can be a serious illness, and some people have had phenomenal success taking medications, such as Prozac. Ask your doctor about the benefits and risks of taking such drugs. Know there is hope.

- If embarrassment or shame overwhelms you, consider looking closely at your self-esteem. Many books on the market address overcoming low self-esteem. Learn to see all of yourself, see life as a continuous process of self-improvement, and laugh at your perceived short-comings. After all, we all have them.

     Read all you can about increasing your self-esteem and self-worth. Learn to honor each part of yourself — the "good," the "bad," the parts you like, and the parts you intend to change.

- If your guilt involves another person, a poignant way to overcome guilt is to apologize to the person we may have hurt. Opening up to the person we hurt fosters understanding, acknowledgment, and compassion. From there, healing is possible and forgiveness and love.

Try a variety of methods to move through your negativity. Know that by being stuck in a negative state, we have no room for healing, forgiveness, love, and happiness. Within negativity, our energy converges on pain, rather than joy.

In life, we all encounter a range of sentiments — love, sorrow, anxiety, fun, happiness, loneliness, loss, depression, exhilaration, pain, pleasure, ecstasy. This range of emotion is our humaneness and what distinguishes us from other mammals. Feel all you were meant to feel. See the messages behind your negativity and use them to heal the past, confront your deepest fears, and move on to extraordinary joy.

Without negativity, we sleep better, feel better, and we are more open to experiencing joy. The faster you overcome negativity, the more energy you have to focus on the essential aspects of life — those that fill you with pleasure.

8
STEP 8
CONFRONT FEAR

We are going to spend this section of our book addressing a specific negative emotion — fear. Fear is the root of many of our problems in life, and it is important we give this issue special attention.

Fear is assuming that what you want or need to have happen will not happen. It is sensing danger on the horizon and anticipating the worst. Fear often paralyzes us, as we lose the courage to act, make decisions, or move forward.

Since fear is focused on what could or might happen to us, it is projecting into and anticipating the future. Fear is a symbol that we are living life not in the present — but in the future. We imagine the future — and a bleak one at that!

In *"Feel the Fear and Do It Anyway,"* Dr. Susan Jeffers suggests that fear can hold us in a position of pain, paralysis, or depression.[26] Often, fear holds us captive and prevents us from experiencing love and joy. It prevents us from accomplishing what we need in life. When fearful, we do not act from a position of self-knowledge, love, and acceptance. Our actions live out anxiety, rather than faith.

We question our instincts. We take ourselves away from natural order because we hesitate. We remain still rather than move forward. We stay in a state of pain and negativity.

When experiencing fear, many of us are skilled at justifying our apprehension. We sight concrete examples of instances where our fears came true. I remember a friend justifying his fear. His company had been purchased through an aggressive acquisition, and he was afraid he would lose his job.

"Every person I know involved in a buy-out lost his job," he said. "I am afraid. It's going to happen to me. And, if it does, I'm going to lose my house. I won't be able to pay my bills. This is devastating!"

My friend justified his anxiety with what he saw as facts. He was convinced that what he had heard as truth — that all people involved in mergers get fired — would come true. He was convinced it was going to happen to him.

We all do this. The fear seems so real. Because we are afraid and to protect ourselves from harm, we develop anger, sadness, depression, frustration, worry, or guilt. To prevent ourselves from enduring pain — facing our fears — we blame other people, pity ourselves, live in disappointment, or harbor guilt.

Let's look at a case to illustrate this point.

The Case of Theresa

Theresa is angry with her husband, Jake. Jake has played golf for three Saturdays in a row, while Theresa cared for their two children. Each day, Jake was gone from 9 a.m. until 3 p.m.

Theresa is beginning to harbor anger toward Jake. He comes home that Friday night and mentions he is considering playing golf again this Sunday. A friend invited him to a prestigious course, and he would like to accept the offer.

Theresa listens and considers Jake's request. She thinks to herself — "This is so unfair! I've watched the children three weekends in a row. When is my break?"

In spite of her feelings, Theresa agrees. "Sure, honey, you can go. Enjoy yourself. No problem. I'll handle the kids." Deep down, she is furious.

After Jake's day of golf, he comes home and says he is tired. He wants to watch television and relax. Meanwhile, Theresa is really fuming inside.

Theresa is angry, hurt, and feels taken advantage of. She resents Jake's ability to take free time when we wants or needs it. She holds this anger inside and it builds and builds.

While anger is on the surface of Theresa's negativity, fear is at the core. Deep down, Theresa is afraid. If you were to ask Theresa about her anger, the conversation might go as follows:

Why are you angry, Theresa?	Because my husband has golfed four weekends this month. I need a break. I need help!
Why are you angry at him?	Because he is taking advantage of me. He should help me with the children.

What if he didn't help?	He made the decision to have children just as I did. He should take responsibility for that decision — with me!
What if he doesn't?	Then he is not the person I thought he was.
And, if he isn't?	Then he is someone else, and I married the wrong person!
You thought you married someone who cared about children as much as you.	Yes.
And, he does not.	I guess not.

Theresa is both angry and fearful. She is afraid that if her husband is taking advantage of her — hurting her — he doesn't really love her. She is afraid she married the wrong person.

Fear is always the basis of our negative thoughts and emotions. You might not know it, but when you are angry, frustrated, worried, or feeling embarrassed, you are really fearful deep down.

Here's another example. Your boss asks you to attend a noteworthy meeting at the office. At the start of the meeting, the chair asks everyone to introduce themselves and asks you to begin.

You introduce yourself. "Hello, everyone, I'm so-and-so. I work in the such-and-such department at such-and-such company. I live in such-and-such area of the city, and I work part-time, three days per week. I have three children — ages 10, 12, and 16."

The person next to you begins. He states his name, title, and company affiliation. Then, the next person goes, and she says her name and company. Then, the next person goes and she just says her name, company, and title. And so on. Everyone after you simply states their name, their position, and their company.

You are embarrassed. You misunderstood what the chairperson meant by introduction and revealed too much detail about yourself. Your embarrassment prevents you from participating in the meeting. Instead, you rehash the mistake in your mind. You feel stupid and shameful.

Let's find the underlying fear.

Why are you embarrassed?	Because I made a fool of myself in front of my colleagues.
How did you do that?	I revealed too much about myself. I talk too much. I'm too open to people, especially my colleagues.
And what if you did?	I made a mistake. People will think I'm stupid.
And what if people think you are stupid?	They might not like or respect me.
And if they don't?	I will be looked down upon.

At the core of this woman's embarrassment is worry that others will not like or respect her. She is ashamed, embarrassed, and afraid.

The method we used to uncover the underlying fear in these examples was developed by David D. Burns in *The Feeling Good Handbook*. Called the Vertical Arrow Technique, Burns recommends writing down your thoughts about a situation that's upsetting you until you reach the core of your negativity.

Once you have written down what is upsetting you, ask yourself the question — if this thought were true, why would it upset me?[27] Keep asking the question until you cannot answer it any differently. In doing so, you will uncover the fear buried within.

Besides the fear of making mistakes and the fear that people will not like us, many of us share other common fears. Among people's greatest anxieties are:

- Fear of height, flying
- Fear of having no money
- Fear of what other people think
- Fear of getting married, commitment, having children
- Fear of failure or not being successful
- Fear of public speaking
- Fear of losing control
- Fear of pain, death or losing a loved one

What Causes Fear?

When fearful, the danger or pain we are avoiding is always the same. All fear is based on the real or imagined fear of being left alone — losing love and human connection. That dread of being left alone when in need is the essence of every dread we hold. It is what holds us back from being all we can be in life.

In *"Attaining Inner Peace,"* Gerald Jampolsky puts forth this revolutionary insight. He says:

> "When you are afraid, no matter what you
> think you fear, the underlying fear you
> have is always the loss of love and
> human connection."[28]

Consider this statement carefully — *all fear is the fear of loss of love and human connection.* Consider the worst terror you can imagine, then see if this statement holds true.

The worst fear I can imagine is death. None of us knows for sure what will happen after we die. For some, religion provides an answer to this lifelong question. For others, the thought that we will feel nothing — no pain, no sorrow — helps allay the fear.

My anxiety over death has held me in paralysis at points in my life. A few years ago, I could not live life to its fullest because I was afraid to die. I was afraid to take chances. I was afraid to fail. I was afraid I was going to die and that my life had no meaning. Like many of us, I had to face my fears and encounter my ultimate demise.

After thinking long and hard about how fear is really fear of loss of love and human connection — fear of separation — I had a wonderful revelation. I realized why I worried so much about death. Some people are afraid to die because of the pain they will endure. Others tremble because the outcome is unknown — what happens after we die?

For me, pain and the unknown were not issues. After all, I survived giving birth, which is the worst pain I could imagine. And, my philosophy has always been — why worry about what you cannot control?

For me, my anxiety over death was based on the belief that if I died, *I would never see the people I loved again.* I realized that if someone promised me that I would see my family and friends after I died — wherever afterlife was — the anxiety subsided.

The loss of love and connection with people I cared about was the essence of my fear, not death itself. And, for every frightful situation I imagined, I concluded the loss of love and human connection was at the core.

Let's look at some examples to see how all fear relates to loss of human connection and love. We will start with the fear of flying and use Burn's Vertical Arrow Technique to uncover the deepest fear within.

You might say unequivocally: "I am afraid of flying. Whenever I go on an airplane, I get an anxiety attack. I feel overwhelmed by fear." Now, ask yourself: "What might happen if I fly? What would upset me?" Possible answers follow.

Question	Answer
What might happen if I fly?	The plane might crash.
What might happen if it crashes?	It might land in the ocean.
What might happen if the plane crashes in the ocean?	I could drown.
What will happen if I drown?	I will die.
What will happen if I die?	My life will be over.

This exercise revealed several surprising facts. This person is not only afraid to fly — she's afraid the plane will crash in the ocean, and she will drown. She is afraid of drowning, and she is afraid of dying. If someone were to reassure her that the plane would not crash, would she be afraid to fly? Maybe yes, maybe no.

Let's look at another fear: "I am afraid to climb ladders."

Question	Answer
What might happen if I climb ladders?	I might fall.
What might happen if I fall?	I might hurt myself.
What might happen if I hurt myself?	No one will be around to help me.

The real fear is being hurt and alone.

Another fear: "I am afraid of losing my job because I have a mortgage to pay and children to take care of."

Question	Answer
What might happen if I lose my job?	I won't be able to pay my mortgage.
What might happen if I can't pay my mortgage?	I will lose my house.
What might happen if I lose my house?	I will have to move in with my parents.
What might happen then?	My parents won't respect me.
What might happen if my parents don't respect me.	They might not love me.

The real fear is that the parents might not love her if she fails.

One more fear: "I am afraid of losing my job because I have a mortgage to pay and children to take care of."

Question	Answer
What might happen if I lose my job?	I won't be able to care for my children.
What might happen if I cannot care for my children?	I will have to go on welfare.
What might happen if I go on welfare?	People might not respect me.
What might happen if people don't respect me.	They might not love me.

The real fear is that people might not love him if he fails.

And another fear: "I am afraid to marry Jane."

Question	Answer
What might happen if I marry?	We might divorce.
And if we divorce?	My parents will be mad.
And if they are mad?	They might be mad at me.
What if they are mad at you?	They might not love me.

Again, the real fear is lost love.

Can you see from the examples above that just about every fear you hold ultimately leads to an underlying fear of losing love?

From this theory, a life philosophy surfaces. In life, you are either acting from a position of fear — worry about tomorrow — or acting from a position of love — knowing that no matter what happens, you will be loved.

The two extremes — fear or love — cannot exist simultaneously.[29] When acting from a position of fear, we create hurt, doubt, unworthiness, solitude, sorrow, and pain. When acting from a position of love, we create healing, self-confidence, worthiness, comradeship, joy, and peace. Since fear and love cannot coexist, when fearful, we cannot love and when loving, we cannot be fearful. To love, we must let go of our fears. When in love, we risk that the love will die or the person will leave us. Love is risk and facing our ultimate fear. Self-love is acting on our instincts without fear. We follow our inner-self with faith and trust. Fear ceases to exist and love takes over.

So, what can we do? What can help us face our anxiety and move forward? How do we overcome fear to reach for true and total self-fulfillment, love, and joy?

Characteristics of Fear

Before confronting fear, we must fully comprehend the phenomenon. As we discussed, all negativity is fear, and inherent in all fear is an unfathomable fear of loss of human connection and love.

Fear possesses other characteristics that will help in our transcending it. First, fear is looking into the future, and so it is imagined.

We imagine that if an action harmed us before, it will again. We imagine that if another person was harmed, the same harm will come to us. We assume the past repeats itself.

Fear is a thought, and we have the ability to change our thoughts.

While watching television one day, I happened upon a show filming a mountain climber. I caught the program just as the climber was ascending a cliff. Afraid of heights, I watched on the edge of my seat as the climber navigated the mountain, step by step.

Then, it happened — the climber fell! She lost her footage and slipped, falling 20 feet before a security rope jerked her back into the mountain's facade. After composing herself, the climber positioned her feet for another ascension.

I couldn't believe what I saw. This woman was not afraid or, if she was, she did not let her fear paralyze her from climbing the mountain she so desperately wanted to master.

I, on the other hand, have always been terrified of height, and this anxiety has prevented me from doing what I need and want to do. As long as I can remember, for example, I have longed to search through my mother's attic. To do so, I have to climb a ladder.

Each time I attempt to confront this fear, I get the same result. I climb four rungs of the ladder and stop. I look up, look down. I imagine the worst: "I'm going to fall." Then, I change my mind. My brother, on the other hand, positions the ladder, climbs it in 30 seconds, and spends hours fishing around the attic.

I know my fear of height is in my mind. If a woman can climb a mountain, facing fear, and if my brother can climb to my mother's attic, why can't I? The trauma lies within me, and I have the power to overcome it.

Another characteristic of fear that we must acknowledge is that fear often stops us from acting. The danger seems so intense, we cannot act and cannot move forward.

While acknowledging fear's ability to paralyze, Dr. Susan Jeffers also gives us hope that anxiety can move us to a place of power.[30] She recommends facing what we dread, rather than waiting for the terror to go away. Sensing fear, facing it, and doing the task in spite of our fear, will help us transcend it.

Overcoming Fear

When fearful, we can try a number of techniques to move through the emotion. Our options include:

- Facing fear head on. Imagining our worst fear, or moving through the fear by taking small steps or bold action.
- Rationalizing away the fear. Reflecting on why we are afraid, looking at facts, and diminishing the fear.
- Counteracting the physical symptoms of fear by meditating or engaging in relaxation techniques.
- Sharing our apprehension with others.

Let's look at each of these options in more detail.

One efficient way to confront fear is to face it in whatever way you feel comfortable. For some, that means diving right in. For others, it means taking small steps. For still others, it means visualizing the horror, then taking necessary action.

If jumping into the fear is your style, the best method is to close your eyes, muster the courage, and dive right in. As Nike® says, "Just do it." Two feet first. Act completely on impulse, without considering the consequences. Know in your heart that you will address the mess later, if any mess results!

Some of us move at a slower pace. Slicing down your fear into smaller, more manageable, less dreadful steps is a good way to approach anxiety. If you are afraid to leave your job, you might start by moving to part-time. Cut your hours from 40 to 30, still being eligible for benefits. Once comfortable with that move, cut back even more to 20 hours or less. These small steps might give you the courage to leave completely.

Visualization is a great way to confront anxiety. Close your eyes, imagine the worst that could happen. Put yourself at the threshold of fear and confront it in your mind.

The Case of Stephen

In his late 20s, Stephen had never been married, although he had developed several meaningful relationships with women over the years. He was committed on serious levels — such as monogamy or living together — but, when it came to marriage, Stephen's anxiety kicked in.

Stephen was about to face a significant decision and one of his greatest fears. He had been dating a terrific woman, Karen, for some time, and Karen had been hinting about her desire to marry. Just the other day, Karen told Stephen she was tired of waiting. She wanted to move their relationship forward or move on. She delivered Stephen an ultimatum. Either they married, or she was going to move on with her life.

Stephen loved Karen immensely and wanted to marry her. He told several friends Karen was "the one" for him. He wanted to face his anxiety over commitment. And, he wanted to do it now, before he lost Karen.

When asked why he was afraid of marriage, Stephen said he feared:

- *That his marriage would not work out*
- *That he would divorce*
- *That his wife would leave him*
- *That his wife would die*
- *That he would lose friends because of the divorce*
- *That he would divorce and could not care for children (if they had any) alone*

With the help of a facilitator, Stephen visualized his worst fears. He imagined fighting with Karen uncontrollably over children and money. He visualized a bitter, painful divorce. He saw himself signing divorce papers and saying good-bye to his wife. In his mind, Stephen lived through the events as if they were real.

Afterward, Stephen felt relief. He came to terms with the possibility of divorce, concluding that although it would be painful, he would survive. He accepted that it might happen and concluded that his imagination was getting away from him. "All this hype," he said, "and it might never happen!"

He also visualized his other deep terrors — that his wife might leave him and that she might die. Using his imagination, Stephen faced the reality of abandonment. He faced losing love.

Stephen also confronted the reality that if his marriage failed, he might lose friendships and love associated with those friendships. He realized true friendships would survive change. He concluded that friendships that do not survive were meant to end.

By addressing all these underlying fears, Stephen overcame his very real anxiety of loss and marriage. He confronted some of his greatest and most profound fears. Then, he was able to move forward. He is now happily married — to Karen!

Besides visualization, another way to confront anxiety is to relax your way through it. Fear has a physical component, where our stomachs get upset, our palms sweat, our heart beats faster, and our minds race. We can counter the physical symptoms of fear by breathing — slowing down our minds and our body.

Try meditating around a fear or relaxing as you step forward into the fear. If facing an upcoming meeting concerns you, take deep breaths before entering the room to calm your body, your mind, and your spirit. Before a stressful confrontation, relax and meditate on the problem. See if calming your mind and your body helps to allay the terror.

Besides facing your anxieties, you could look at the facts to pacify your fears. Fear often clouds our reasoning and looking at facts can sometimes allay our anxiety.

In examining the facts, we might conclude our worries are not based on reality, but our imagination. We might see that other people faced the same anxiety, confronted it, and the outcome was positive. We might realize that the past does not always repeat itself.

Another effective way to confront fear is to share your anxiety with a friend or family member. Remember, *loss of love is at the root of all fear*. Sharing with others establishes a link, countering the possibility of loss of human connection.

Sharing also can be a source of strength or ideas. Some people may have already faced the very fear you dread. They can tell you the result of their actions or how they moved forward. You might even decide to face the fear together. In company, there is peace.

So, now you are equipped with a number of techniques to confront your fear. As you begin to master fear more and more acutely, your ability to take risks, make decisions, and take on new challenges will improve.

But, what about people who live their lives seemingly fearless? What about people who dare to be who they truly are without any thought of failure or how people view them? What about people who blindly follow their instincts, with no concern over the outcome? Can you become one of those people?

If all fear is ultimately fear of loss of human connection and love, what would happen if we faced that most extreme terror head on? If we were to overcome the fear of separation, would all lesser fears disappear? If we accepted that we are, and will always be, all alone in life, would we be more open to experiencing joy?

It is true, you know, that we are all alone in life. We come into life alone — as an infant navigating the birth channel and being swept away by a doctor once our body emerges. We die alone, as our breath is taken away from us, and our body's nervous system fails to feel pain or joy.

What if we were completely banished from seeing our loved ones? What if we were all alone to face our life's challenges? What if we were:

Alone and homeless   Alone and hungry

EXERCISE 16 — The Roots of Fear

Take time now to consider what scares you. Think of all aspects of your life — your career, your family, spirituality, and your leisure time. What causes you anxiety? When are you most stressed and why?

Pick one idea, thing, or person that scares you and pinpoint the underlying fear associated with it, using Burn's Vertical Arrow Technique. Can you find the link between your anxiety and loss of love?

Now, reflect on how you confronted fear in the past. What is your fear-busting style? Have you jumped into your fears? broken them into small steps? visualized them? Do you like to have facts at your disposal? Are you comfortable sharing your fears with others?

Consider someone you know who is fearless in his or her approach to life. Reflect on this person's characteristics. Is she a risk-taker? Does she worry? Does she trust? How do you feel when you spend time with this person? What could you learn from her?

The next time you fear an action, what will you do to face it? What did you learn about fear in this section of the book, and how do you feel about fear now?

Alone and terrorized   Alone and scared
Alone and broke   Alone and in pain
Alone and sick   Alone and dieing?
Alone and tortured

What if we faced these very real and intense fears? Would all our lesser fears disappear? Would we live life fearlessly?

Or, does love counter all. Does self-love make being alone all right, after all? Does loving others link us and alleviate our ever being alone?

Whether you are ready to face your ultimate fear of being alone, know that you invent terror, and you can eliminate it. Know that overcoming anxiety takes trust. Know that the first fear you overcome will be your hardest and that as you confront fears, one-by-one, your ability to do so strengthens. Through practice, you can learn to identify and conquer anxiety keenly.

To ultimately conquer apprehension, trust your instincts without speculating about the unknown. Live in the moment and forget the future.

Know that by confronting fear, real joy can open up to you. We cannot give if we fear being without. We cannot love without acknowledging that love may end. We cannot live fully without confronting inevitable death.

No matter how deeply you look within to find your anxieties or how you chose to address them, the process of doing so will invigorate you and lead you to a more pleasurable life.

9
STEP 9
ACKNOWLEDGE YOUR NEED
TO CONNECT

Mammals travel in packs or herds, and humans, as mammals, are naturally social beings. We find safety in numbers, knowing we are members of a larger human race, which is more powerful than ourselves in solitude. We also find security in knowing other people share our same fears and face similar challenges.

The need for human contact is intensely strong but that calling does not mean a person cannot be happy alone. I love being alone and use time with myself to engage in activities that bring me immense joy. I walk in the woods, read books I love, meditate, or exercise. I often work alone. I love the solitude, the control, and the quietness.

The desire for human contact also does not mean that a person without a love partner or long-term relationship cannot be happy. Many people confuse sexual relations with intimacy. Some even define intimacy as sex. Intimacy does not come from human physical contact. Instead, intimacy fosters through sharing of oneself with others. Intimacy, then, can manifest itself between friends, parents and children, co-workers, and siblings, as well as life partners.

In *The Pursuit of Happiness*, David G. Myers, Ph.D., points out that people who share themselves with others — extroverts — are more happy with life than people who do not. He says, "In study after study, extroverts — sociable, outgoing people — report greater happiness and satisfaction with life."[31]

Extroverts are happier partly because they have self-confidence and like themselves. Myers says: "Self-assured people who walk into a room full of strangers and warmly introduce themselves may also be more accepting of themselves. Liking themselves, they are confident that others will like them, too. And such attitudes tend to be self-fulfilling, leading extroverts to experience more positive events."[32]

Myers goes on to say that extroverts are more involved with

people, have a larger circle friends, and greater social support. They also experience more affection.[33]

Why is association with others so intertwined with joy? First, we must realize that belonging is a basic human need. "Belongingness" is the third tier on Maslow's hierarchy of basic needs. Our desire for companionship is third only to physical needs and security.

Companionship also allays our fears. As humans, our greatest fear is loss of human connection or loss of love. Through relating to others, we pacify this fear and others less prominent. Sharing eases anxiety and fosters love and joy.

Every step of our Happiness Model involves sharing on some level. Step 3 — honoring others as they are, without judgment — can help us connect better with other people because we seek to understand them, rather than judge them.

Step 6 of the Happiness Model is living in the present, and to do so, we must concentrate on other people when we come in contact with them. Talking with another person, relating one-on-one, is truly living and being present. Through this concentration on another's feelings, aspirations, and challenges, we can emphasize and connect on a deeper level.

We overcome negativity more keenly when we open up to others. One method of confronting anger, disappointment, guilt, and worry is to discuss these feelings with another person. Self-expression fosters healing, as we open ourselves up and see that others share our pain and challenges.

Connecting, then, is essential in every step of our Happiness Model. We all require time and association with others. No matter how strong or independent we are, we need people. We need intimacy and love. We need to feel part of a larger community. These needs are a thread that weaves itself throughout all of our challenges in becoming a more joyous person.

If you lack companionship in your life, you might be acting from your position of ultimate fear — fear of separation. Often we are afraid to show our true self to others because we visualize their rejection. Instead of facing the terror, we recoil. After all, if you retract, how can someone reject you?

Instead of sharing ourselves and facing exclusion — we remain introverted. As a result, we suffer loneliness, solitude, and addiction, which keeps our true self concealed.

If the thought of waiting until tomorrow to join with people occurs to you, I would encourage you to step out today. Tomorrow might never come. Something could happen to you or to the other person. Do not delay the most stirring duty in life — to share love.

If you have trouble associating with others, reread the nine steps to happiness outlined in this book. Practice STEP 1 — Commit today to increasing your happiness. By committing to and sharing your experiences with others, real love and, therefore, real happiness will come into your life.

You might be waiting for someone else to share before you open to them. If so, I would refer you to STEP 2 — take control of your life and your happiness. You are in the driver's seat. As you reveal yourself, others will return that openness to you.

If you consider yourself right and other people wrong, or if you want people to change before you connect with them — read STEP 3. Honor others and the world as they are and it is, without judgment. You are not the judge. Let others live with their decisions, and you live with yours. Open up anyway.

If you consistently avoid contact with others, I would remind you of STEP 4 — recognize your basic need to belong. We all have it, and you are not exempt.

Too busy to call a friend or talk to a member of your family? I would refer you to STEP 5 and suggest you realign your commitments to make room for others. Realign what you do in life to fulfill your needs. Companionship is the only way to gratify your need to belong with others and a larger communion.

If you say to yourself that you will call that friend or talk to that neighbor tomorrow — I would refer you to STEP 6 — live in the present. Tomorrow might never come. Do it today.

If you are mad, and if that anger prevents you from stepping out into the world and associating with someone, see STEP 7 — confront negativity. If you are frustrated, saddened by another person's actions, or worried about them, pick up the phone. Express your anger, frustration, sadness, or worry. Forgive and heal. Put the negativity behind you and replace it with love.

If you are afraid to associate with others, if rejection haunts you, I would refer you to STEP 8 — know that everyone finds terror in separation. Step out of that fear. Take small steps. Visualize your fear. Relax through it. Look at the facts. Then, just do it. Pick up the phone or knock at the door.

Finally, if you think you can survive in this world alone, see STEP 9 and acknowledge your desire to belong. Happiness cannot occur in a lonely vacuum. Sharing and being with others will surely intensify your pleasure.

Being An Energy Person

The world contains what have been termed "toxic" people and energy people. Toxic people are people who bring us down — who depress us. They are victims who have yet to take charge of their lives. Selfish and self-centered, they lack joy and suck pleasure from others.

Energy people, on the other hand, live actively. They take charge of their lives and their happiness. They know and address their needs, and they live for now. They have strength, and they pass that strength onto others through their interactions and work. They do not harbor negative feelings — they express them, face them, and move on. They are open to and are careful of judgment toward others.

I would encourage you to become an energy person and spend as much time as possible with energy people. As an energy person, you become a catalyst for joining a community together in harmony. You are a source of energy and joy.

You might choose to limit your time with toxic people. Realize that you cannot help toxic people take charge of their life. That choice is theirs to make. You can support them, but know that you govern your life, and you can walk away from the conversation at any time. Above all, let no one else bring you down!

The Case of Bernard

A 38-year-old single man, Bernard was hardworking, attractive, and successful. Although his family background was a challenge — his father was an alcoholic and his mother suffered from manic depression — Bernard had managed to pick himself up in life.

Occasionally, however, Bernard found himself sinking into depression. And, throughout the years, Bernard had shown signs of having a drinking problem himself. He also was a self-proclaimed workaholic. Working made him feel good, he said. He felt in control, successful, and challenged. Work brought him immense joy.

His personal life lacked intimacy. He had one close friend, and many of his other connections with people came from work. He took advantage of work functions as a way to meet and talk with people. Outside work, Bernard had few friends.

Most recently, Bernard started to date a woman from the office. They courted seven months when the relationship abruptly ended. In talking about the demise of the partnership, Bernard said his com-

panion could not handle a serious relationship. As they grew closer, she became afraid and distant.

The breakup devastated Bernard. He found himself in a deep depression.

I worked with Bernard also and frequently met him in the hallway or the coffee room, as our offices were close to one another. He enjoyed discussing his love situation with me. I was a good ear. It had been six months since the breakup, and Bernard was still rehashing the past.

One conversation went like this: "Do you think I should call her? I want to call her so badly. The other day I was sitting at home by the phone. I debated picking up the phone. Do you think she will think I'm desperate if I call? Do you think she's dating someone else?"

Each time I spoke with Bernard, my heart filled with sorrow. After six months, he had not resolved this relationship, and he needed help.

Simultaneously, I was conscious of my own needs. I did not want to be drawn into the negativism that was his life. I did not want to spend my time complaining and receiving his toxic energy.

One day, while Bernard and I were talking, I noticed my mind was elsewhere. I was not present to him.

Then, I turned my attention toward him and really listened. As I centered on his words, I realized that what he was saying made sense to me. I had similar frustrations and had lived through profound sadness in my life. I had looked to others for joy or criticism. I had gone home to an empty house, afraid to interact with others. I had been hurt by a long-lost love. I had been there, too.

My frustration with Bernard and my inability to hear him ceased. Instead, I was able to relate to him and, through empathy, he reminded me how far I have come. My interactions with Bernard became a source of strength and confidence for me and gave him a caring message.

How to Connect

How do you do it? How do you make human contact a part of your daily life? Where do you meet people? How do you foster intimacy?

Opportunities to share come to us each and every day of our lives. Set aside time each day to converse with your co-workers, your friends, your family, and people on the street. Every encounter with another human being — in the grocery store, on the train, paying a toll on the highway — gives us an opportunity to join with the human race. These are opportunities to spread joy.

Once a week or every few days, call a friend and talk for 10 minutes, 15 minutes — whatever time you can spare. If you put comradeship on the calendar, you are more likely to participate. Turn off the television. Turn off the radio. Put this book — and other books down. Stop working. Stop shopping. Talk to a neighbor. Pick up the phone and say "hi." Be and do together.

When you connect, put your whole true self out there, without embarrassment or worry about what others will think. Express yourself and relate experiences without embarrassment. Face your fear of rejection. Know that some people will find your way strange and different. In that though, they can discover ways to open themselves up to the variety that is human nature.

Remember, sharing love does not mean marriage, a lifelong companion, or a love interest. You do not have to be married to share intimately with other people. If you are single, seek intimacy through friendships, co-workers, family, and neighbors. Waiting for a love interest to participate in intimacy with others might be a long wait, indeed.

At times in my life, I have felt more intimate and close to friends than to my husband. Other times, my husband has been a wonderful source of closeness. My family — my sisters and my mother — often serves as a primary source of companionship. I share intimacy with many people in my life, not just my husband.

Remember, too, that self-love is a form of intimacy and a source of love. Get to know yourself — your true, authentic self. Developing a clear and solid sense of yourself is one way to confront our fear of rejection. When we love ourselves unconditionally, rejection from others does not matter so much. We see ourselves as whole, in and with ourselves.

When you seek love outside yourself — from a parent, a spouse, a friend, a sibling, or a neighbor — the other person can take love away at any moment. That person could reject you — she could move out of town, or die. When we love from within, however, it is stable, consistent, and long-lasting.

Through unconditional self-love, we learn to love others unconditionally. As we express and show love to others, they are more likely to desire spending time with us. Sharing our thoughts, activities, and life with others fosters infinite happiness.

Be all you can and desire to be. Love yourself in spite of your perceived faults and challenges. Take care of your self. Know you have value. Then, associate genuinely and sincerely with others.

Part of loving yourself and loving others is seeing our and their entire being — likes, dislikes, faults, strengths, desperation, and joy. All of us exist somewhere on the happiness continuum. Some of us are a little further along, and some of us have a way to go. Each of us, though, struggles with the potential for reaching true joy.

Involve yourself in the lives of others and share yourself without worry. Make associating with others a priority in your life. Be friendly. Open yourself up. Recognize that you have thoughts and experiences to share.

Become a person of energy. The more power you have within you, the more you can give to others. The more you give, the more you get back. This energy cycle feeds on itself and can be a positive force in your life.

EXERCISE 17 — Relating to Others

On a scale of 1 to 5, how would you rate your ability to relate to others, with one being NEEDS IMPROVEMENT and 5 being EXEMPLARY. How would you rate others close to you? Who can you identify who ranks 1, and who ranks 5?

Consider the person ranking 1. What do you suppose this person fears? How would you recommend this person overcome this fear? What could you do to help him feel less fearful?

Consider the person you ranked 5. What characteristics does this person possess? What do you suppose this person fears, and how does he confront it?

If you were to face rejection as a way to conquer fear of connecting, how would you approach it? Do you share openly now? If you were to share openly with others, what would you say?

Do you see a correlation between fear, sharing, and happiness? Define that correlation. Where is your commitment to connecting sincerely with other people? How essential is companionship to your joy? What can you do from now on to add human contact to your life?

The Universe Connects Us

As we touch others, we become less self-centered. We recognize that we are not alone in this world, and this fosters intimacy and peace. We realize that others share the same feelings and desires as we — the same challenges — in varying degrees.

Society needs you. You have an essential role in this world and in the movement of the universe. You might not know what that role is, but it exists and it is truth. People deserve to see you and know you. The world needs you — the whole you, just the way you are.

Ultimately, however, it is not about you and your happiness. Sharing with others has little to do with you, though it might make you feel better. Opening to others is about giving. Giving love.

Renowned orator and philosopher Marianne Williamson says it best in *Marianne Williamson on Self-Esteem*. She uses people speaking into a microphone at her workshops to illustrate her point. Many people fear talking into a microphone since their voice carries throughout the auditorium. Williamson reminds them — "It's not about you."[34]

When you speak — in public or one-to-one — it's not about you at all. When you give of yourself and express yourself fully — it's about others. It's about the people to whom you are speaking. You have an obligation to speak. You have an obligation to be yourself and share yourself with the universe.

The universe needs you. Share it all. Share your ear. Share your experiences. Share advice. Share guidance. Share your thoughts. Share time. Share gifts. Share greetings. Share notes. Share a kiss. Share love.

And see all you get back exponentially in return.

REFERENCES

[1] David G. Myers, Ph.D., *The Pursuit of Happiness. Who is Happy — And Why*. William Morrow and Company, New York, N.Y. 1992.

[2] Mihaly Csikszentmihalyi. *Finding Flow. The Psychology of Engagement with Everyday Life*. Basic Books, New York, N.Y. 1997. Page 32.

[3] John B. Baucom, Ph.D. *Baby Steps to Happiness. 52 inspiring ways to make your life happy*.   Starburst Publisher, Lancaster, PA. 1996. Page 135.

[4] Baucom. Page 76.

[5] Baucom. Page 76.

[6] Dr. Spencer Johnson. *The Precious Present*. Doubleday, Garden City, N.Y. 1984. Page 65.

[7] John Roger and Peter McWilliams. *Life 101. Everything We Wish We Had Learned in School — But Didn't*.   Prelude Press, Los Angeles, CA. 1991. Page 105.

[8] Baucom. Page 149.

[9] Sarah Ban Breathnach, *Simple Abundance*. Warner Books, N.Y., N.Y. 1995. October 3.

[10] Marianne Williamson. *Marianne Williamson on Self-Esteem*. (audio cassette) Harper Audio, New York, N.Y. 1992.

[11] Landmark Education, Inc. *The Forum* (workshop). Philadelphia, PA. July 1996.

[12] Abraham H. Maslow. *Motivation and Personality*. Third Edition. Harper & Row, New York, NY. 1954. Pages 15-22.

[13] Maslow.

[14] Maslow.

15 Maslow.

16 Wendy Swallow Williams. *Ladies' Home Journal.* January 1997. Page 146.

17 Csikszentmihalyi. Page 30-35.

18 Csikszentmihalyi. Page 30-35.

19 Baucom. Page 135.

20 Landmark Education.

21 Dr. Susan J. Jeffers. *Feel the Fear and Do It Anyway* (audio cassette). Nightingale-Conant Corporation. 1988.

22 Dr. John Gray, Ph.D. Seen on "The Oprah Winfrey Show". September 1998.

23 Dr. John Gray, Ph.D. *Men are From Mars, Women Are From Venus. A practical guide for improving communication and getting to know what you want in your relationships.* Harper Collins, New York, N.Y. 1992. Page 208-218. Reprinted with permission from the author, September 1998.

24 Michael D. Yapko, Ph.D. *Breaking Patterns of Depression.* Doubleday, New York, N.Y. 1997. Page 155-157.

25 Yapko. Page 214.

26 Jeffers

27 David D. Burns M.D., *The Feeling Good Handbook. Using the new mood therapy in everyday life.* William Morrow, N.Y. 1989. Page 122-23.

28 Gerald Jampolsky and Diane V. Cirincione. *Attaining Inner Peace* (audio cassette). Simon & Schuster Audio, N.Y. 1993.

29 Jampolsky and Cirincione.

30 Jeffers.

[31] Myers. Page 120.

[32] Myers. Page 120.

[33] Myers. Page 121.

[34] Williamson.

SUMMARY OF EXERCISES

EXERCISE 1 —   Identifying Happiness in your Life
EXERCISE 2 —   Examining Happiness in your Life
EXERCISE 3 —   Roadblocks to Your Happiness
EXERCISE 4 —   Your Commitments
EXERCISE 5 —   Clarifying Responsibility
EXERCISE 6 —   Reality Check
EXERCISE 7 —   Defining Perfection
EXERCISE 8 —   Needs and Wants
EXERCISE 9 —   Finding Your Lost Self
EXERCISE 10 —   Your Schedule
EXERCISE 11 —   Your Likes and Dislikes
EXERCISE 12 —   Reviewing Musts and Shoulds
EXERCISE 13 —   Rethinking Your Commitments
EXERCISE 14 —   Being Present
EXERCISE 15 —   Pinpointing Negativity
EXERCISE 16 —   The Roots of Fear
EXERCISE 17 —   Relating to Others

RECOMMENDED READING AND LISTENING

John B. Baucom, Ph.D. *Baby Steps to Happiness. 52 inspiring ways to make your life happy*. Starburst Publisher, Lancaster, PA. 1996.

Sarah Ban Breathnach, *Simple Abundance*. Warner Books, N.Y., N.Y. 1995.

David D. Burns, M.D. *The Feeling Good Handbook. Using the new mood therapy in everyday life*. W. Morrow, N.Y. 1989.

Richard Carlson, Ph.D. *Don't Sweat the Small Stuff; and It's all Small Stuff*. Hyperion, New York, N.Y. 1997.

Deepak Chopra. *The Higher Self* (audio cassette). Simon & Schuster, N.Y. 1993.

Mihaly Csikszentmihalyi. *Flow. The Psychology of Optimal Experience. Steps toward enhancing the quality of life*. Harper and Row, New York, N.Y. 1990.

Wayne W. Dyer. *Your Erroneous Zones*. Funk and Wagnalls. 1976.

Dr. John Gray. *Men are From Mars, Women Are From Venus. A practical guide for improving communication and getting to know what you want in your relationships*. Harper Collins, New York, N.Y. 1992.

Louise L. Hay. *Meditations for Personal Healing* (audio cassette). Hay House. 1993.

Ernest R. Hilgard, Rita L. Atkinson, Richard C. Atkinson. *Introduction to Psychology*, Seventh Edition. Harcourt Brace Jovanovich, Inc., New York, N.Y. 1979.

Gerald Jampolsky and Diane V. Cirincione. *Attaining Inner Peace* (audio cassette). Simon & Schuster Audio, N.Y. 1993.

Dr. Susan J. Jeffers. *Feel the Fear and Do It Anyway* (audio cassette). Nightingale-Conant Corporation. 1988.

Dr. Spencer Johnson. *The Precious Present*. Doubleday, Garden City, N.Y. 1984.

Ken Keyese, Jr., with Penny Keyes. *Your Life is a Gift, So make the Most of It!*, Love Line Books, Coos Bay, OR. 1987.

Landmark Education, Inc. *The Forum* (workshop). Philadelphia, PA. July 1996.

Harriet Goldhor Lerner. *The Dance of Anger. A woman's guide to changing the patterns of intimate relationships*. Harper and Row, N.Y. 1985.

Abraham H. Maslow. *Motivation and Personality*. Harper and Row, N.Y. 1954.

David G. Myers, Ph.D. *The Pursuit of Happiness. Who Is Happy — and Why*. William Morrow and Company, Inc., N.Y. 1992.

Mildred Newman and Bernard Berkowitz with Jean Owen. *How to be Your Own Best Friend*, Ballantine Books, N.Y. 1971

John Roger and Peter McWilliams. *Life 101. Everything We Wish We Had Learned in School — But Didn't*. Prelude Press, Los Angeles, CA. 1991.

Gail Sheehy. *Passages: Predictable Crises of Adult Life*. E. P. Dutton and Company, N.Y. 1976.

Marsha Sinetar. *Do What you Love, the Money will Follow*. Dell Publishing, N.Y. 1987.

Sharon Wedscheider-Cruse. *Learning to Love Yourself. Finding your Self Worth*. Health Communications, Inc., FL. 1987.

Marianne Williamson. *Marianne Williamson on Self-Esteem*. (audio cassette) Harper Audio, New York, N.Y. 1992.
Michael D. Yapko, Ph.D. *Breaking Patterns of Depression*. Doubleday, New York, N.Y. 1997.

ABOUT THE AUTHOR

A writer and marketing executive, Diane M. Kolodzinski has worked in the field of communications for 18 years. As a corporate executive for a major Philadelphia-based bank, Kolodzinski longed to pursue her real love: writing and teaching.

She wrote <u>Reclaiming your Happiness</u> and founded The Happiness Clinic after studying happiness as a phenomenon and turning her own life around. Like most woman, Kolodzinski had experienced low self-esteem and lack of courage to live her dreams.

She saw the possibility of living a more joyous life and developed within her the courage change. She educated herself by reading hundreds of books, listening to self-help tapes, attending workshops, and participating in personal counseling.

<u>Reclaiming your Happiness</u> is the culmination of her research. Kolodzinski says she has been preparing her whole life to write this book. She still uses her model when her life gets "off course."

She says: "Living a life with happiness as your number one goal takes focus and a commitment. Day-to-day activities get in the way of that primary and all-important goal. By concentrating on your joy, you would be amazed at how your life can change."

For more information about having Diane M. Kolodzinski speak on her book, write to:

The Happiness Clinic
70 Guilford Circle
Phoenixville, PA 19460
(610) 935-8033

Or, contact Ms. Kolodzinski on her website at DMKolodzin@aol.com.